COBOL Reference Summary

PUBLISHED BY NCC PUBLICATIONS

British Library Cataloguing in Publication Data

Cobol reference summary. – 2nd ed.
1. COBOL (Computer program language)
001.64'24 QA76.3.C25

ISBN 0-85012-318-6

First published in 1981 by:

NCC Publications, The National Computing Centre Limited,
Oxford Road, Manchester M1 7ED

Typeset in 10pt Press Roman by Focal Design Studios Limited,
New Mills, Stockport, Cheshire

Printed in England by UPS Blackburn Limited

ISBN 0-85012-318-6

Acknowledgments

THE BOOK

The original version of this book was produced internally by NCC. This version is the result of some revision and improvement of the original text by John Triance.

THE LANGUAGE

COBOL is an industry language and is not the property of any company or group of companies, or of any organisation or group of organisations.

No warranty, expressed or implied, is made by any contributor or by the CODASYL Programming Language Committee as to the accuracy and functioning of the programming system and language. Moreover, no responsibility is assumed by any contributor, or by the committee, in connection herewith.

The authors and copyright holders of the copyrighted material used herein

> FLOW-MATIC (trademark of Sperry Rand Corporation), Programming for the UNIVAC® I and II, Data Automation Systems copyrighted 1958, 1959, by Sperry Rand Corporation; IBM Commercial Translator Form No. F 28-8013, copyrighted 1959 by IBM; FACT, DSI 27A5260-2760, copyrighted 1960 by Minneapolis-Honeywell

have specifically authorised the use of this material in whole or in part, in the COBOL specifications. Such authorisation extends to the reproduction and use of COBOL specifications in programming manuals or similar publications.

Contents

1 Introduction

1.1 PURPOSE AND ORGANISATION

The purpose of this reference summary is to provide a clear and concise statement of the COBOL language features, and their effects. It is not intended to be a full reproduction of the ANS 74 standard.

When you are writing programs, and want to know the exact form of a particular type of statement or entry, you can refer to the appropriate section and discover exactly what is permissible, and what the effect of the statement or entry is.

1.2 NOTATION USED IN FORMATS

Formats are represented in the following style

```
{ VALUE IS   }            [ { THROUGH }           ]
{ VALUES ARE }  literal-1 [ { THRU    }  literal-2 ]

                [           [ { THROUGH }           ] ]
                [ literal-3 [ { THRU    }  literal-4 ] ] ...
```

The following conventions are used throughout this book.

Underlined upper case words, eg VALUE, are obligatory reserved words. All such words which appear in the option being used must be written in the position shown in the format.

Upper case words which are not underlined, eg IS, are optional reserved words. They may only be used in the positions shown in the formats but may, at the wish of the programmer, be omitted without any alteration to the meaning of the code.

Braces { }, indicate a choice. The programmer is permitted to write any of the lines within the braces. The meaning of the different alternatives is given in the rules associated with the format. If there is only one line in the braces then it must be written. In this latter case the braces are merely used to help indicate repetition (see ellipsis below).

Brackets [ ] indicate that the entry within the brackets may be included or omitted as required by the programmer.

Note: Brackets and braces may be nested. Thus for example an item in brackets may contain another item enclosed in brackets or braces.

Ellipsis ... indicates that the item which immediately precedes the ellipsis may be repeated as many times as the programmer wishes. If the ellipsis immediately follows a closing bracket or brace then the whole entry in the brackets or braces is repeated. Otherwise the word which immediately precedes the ellipsis is repeated.

Lower case words represent coding which is to be specified by the programmer. Only coding of the type specified, ie literal, data-name, etc, may be specified. Sometimes the coding that may be specified is further restricted by the associated rules.

Note

1. When the same lower case word appears more than once in a format it is suffixed with a unique number so that it can be distinguished in the associated rules.

2. Wherever imperative-statement is used one or more imperative-statements may be written.

1.3 OVERALL STRUCTURE OF COBOL PROGRAMS

Below is a list of the Standard Headings in a COBOL program.

```
IDENTIFICATION DIVISION.
PROGRAM-ID.
AUTHOR.            )
INSTALLATION.      |
DATE-WRITTEN.      }    Optional
DATE-COMPILED.     |
SECURITY.          )

ENVIRONMENT DIVISION.
CONFIGURATION SECTION.
SOURCE-COMPUTER.
OBJECT-COMPUTER.
SPECIAL-NAMES.          Optional
INPUT-OUTPUT SECTION.   Optional – but usually needed
FILE-CONTROL.           Needed if INPUT-OUTPUT SECTION coded
I-O-CONTROL.            Optional – rarely used
```

DATA DIVISION.	
FILE SECTION.	Optional – but usually needed
WORKING–STORAGE SECTION	Optional – but usually needed
LINKAGE SECTION.	Optional
PROCEDURE DIVISION.	

2 Identification Division

2.1 STRUCTURE

<u>IDENTIFICATION</u> <u>DIVISION</u>.

<u>PROGRAM–ID</u>. program–name.

[<u>AUTHOR</u>. comment–entry]

[<u>INSTALLATION</u>. comment–entry]

[<u>DATE–WRITTEN</u>. comment–entry]

[<u>DATE–COMPILED</u>. comment–entry]

[<u>SECURITY</u>. comment–entry]

Rules and Effects

1. The program-name must follow the rules for a user-defined name. (NB as the program name is often used outside the program, it may also have to follow rules specific to the implementation.)
2. All comment-entries are printed as part of the program listing and otherwise ignored by the compiler, except for the entry for DATE–COMPILED. If this entry is specified, then the compiler replaces it on the listing with the date of compilation.
3. Each comment-entry may contain any string of characters and words, spread, if desired, over a number of lines. The precise use made of each entry depends on the programmer (or the installation).
4. Apart from SECURITY the purpose of each paragraph is fairly obvious. The SECURITY paragraph is sometimes used to indicate who is allowed to use, read or amend the program.

3 Environment Division

3.1 STRUCTURE

Format

ENVIRONMENT DIVISION.

CONFIGURATION SECTION.

SOURCE–COMPUTER. computer-name [DEBUGGING MODE clause].

OBJECT–COMPUTER. computer-name [MEMORY SIZE clause].

[SPECIAL–NAMES.[implementor-name clause] ...
[CURRENCY SIGN clause]
[DECIMAL POINT clause]]

[INPUT–OUTPUT SECTION.

FILE–CONTROL.

[SELECT entry] ...]

[I–O-CONTROL.

[SAME clause] ...

[RERUN clause] ...

[MULTIPLE FILE TAPE clause] .... .]

Rules and Effects

1. The format of computer-name is defined by the implementor.
2. The FILE–CONTROL paragraph, and therefore the INPUT–OUTPUT section, is required if any files are to be defined.
3. The I–O–CONTROL paragraph is required if SAME, RERUN or MULTIPLE FILE TAPE clauses are to be given. These clauses are rarely used and are not covered in this book.

3.2 CURRENCY SIGN CLAUSE

Format

CURRENCY SIGN IS literal

Rules

literal must be a non-numeric literal of length 1. It must not be any of the following characters 0 1 2 3 4 5 6 7 8 9 A B C D L P R S V X Z * + – , . ; ( ) " / = or space.

Function and Effect

This clause allows an alternative currency symbol to be used in the PICTURE clause. Whatever character is specified behaves exactly as is described for £ in section 4.14.

3.3 DECIMAL POINT CLAUSE

Format

DECIMAL–POINT IS COMMA

Function and Effect

If this clause is specified, then the functions of the comma and the dot in picture specifications and numeric literals are exchanged.

3.4 DEBUGGING MODE CLAUSE

Format

WITH DEBUGGING MODE

Function and Effect

See debugging lines (section 6.7).

3.5 IMPLEMENTOR–NAME CLAUSE

Format

implementor-name IS mnemonic-name

Rules

The valid implementor-names and their meanings are specified by the implementor.

Function and Effect

This clause is used to define the meaning of mnemonic-name for use in the ACCEPT, DISPLAY and WRITE statements.

3.6 MEMORY SIZE CLAUSE

Format

```
                        { WORDS      }
MEMORY SIZE integer     { CHARACTERS }
                        { MODULES    }
```

Function and Effect

The clause is used to specify the amount of memory space available for the object program. Its effect is implementor-dependent – many compilers treat the clause as comments.

3.7 SELECT ENTRY – INDEXED FILES

Format

```
SELECT file-name
    ASSIGN TO implementor-name ...
  [ RESERVE integer { AREA  } ]
  [                 { AREAS } ]
    ORGANIZATION IS INDEXED
  [                  { SEQUENTIAL } ]
  [ ACCESS MODE IS   { RANDOM     } ]
  [                  { DYNAMIC    } ]
    [RECORD KEY IS data-name-1]
    [ALTERNATE RECORD KEY IS data-name-2 [WITH DUPLICATES] ] ...
    [FILE STATUS IS data-name-3]
```

Rules

1. file-name is the name of the COBOL file which must be later defined in an FD entry.
2. implementor-name varies in its form and meaning from implementation to implementation. It is used to link file-name to the operating system.
3. integer must be greater than zero.

4. data-name-1 and data-name-2 must each be defined as an alphanumeric item in one of the records for this file. They may be qualified.
5. data-name-3 must identify a 2 character alphanumeric item *not* defined in the file section. It may be qualified.

Function and Effect

The SELECT entry names a file and provides at least part of the link between it and the operating system.

If RESERVE is specified then integer areas are provided for processing blocks of data read from or written to the file.

ORGANIZATION IS INDEXED indicates that data records on the file are stored in such a way that they can be accessed sequentially or randomly by their key values.

ACCESS SEQUENTIAL indicates that the records on the file will be processed in ascending key sequence, ACCESS RANDOM indicates that a key value will be specified for every record which it is required to process. ACCESS DYNAMIC indicates that both Sequential and Random processing will occur. If no Access Mode is specified, Sequential is assumed.

RECORD KEY specifies the data item in the record which contains the key value identifying the record.

FILE STATUS specifies the data item in which values indicating the success (or otherwise) of Input/Output operations will be stored. See FILE STATUS, section 3.11.

ALTERNATE RECORD KEY specifies a data item in the record which can be used as an alternative to the record key for randomly accessing records. If WITH DUPLICATES is specified the same key value may appear in more than one record in the file.

3.8 SELECT ENTRY – RELATIVE FILES

Format

```
SELECT file-name
    ASSIGN TO implementor-name ...
  [                 { AREA  } ]
  [ RESERVE integer {       } ]
  [                 { AREAS } ]
    ORGANIZATION IS RELATIVE
  [                 { SEQUENTIAL } ]
  [ ACCESS MODE IS  { RANDOM     } ]
  [                 { DYNAMIC    } ]
    [RELATIVE KEY IS data-name-1]
    [FILE STATUS IS data-name-2]
```

Rules

1. file-name is the name of the COBOL file which must be later defined in an FD entry.
2. implementor-name varies in its meaning from implementation to implementation. It is used to link file-name to the operating system.
3. integer must be greater than zero.
4. data-name-1 must be defined as an unsigned integer *not* in one of the records for this file. It may be qualified.
5. data-name-2 must identify a 2 character alphanumeric item *not* defined in the file section. It may be qualified.

Function and Effect

The SELECT entry names a file and provides at least part of the link between it and the operating system.

If RESERVE is specified then integer areas are provided for processing blocks of data read from or written to the file.

ORGANIZATION IS RELATIVE indicates that data records on the file can be stored and accessed using the Relative Key value.

ACCESS SEQUENTIAL indicates that the records on the file will be processed in ascending key sequence, ACCESS RANDOM indicates that a key value will be specified for every record which it is required to process. ACCESS DYNAMIC indicates that both Sequential and Random processing will occur.

RELATIVE KEY must be specified for ACCESS RANDOM and DYNAMIC. It is optional for SEQUENTIAL. data-name-1 is the data item which will contain the relative number of the record being processed.

The FILE STATUS clause specifies the data item in which values indicating the success (or otherwise) of Input/Output operations will be stored. See FILE STATUS, section 3.11.

3.9 SELECT ENTRY – SEQUENTIAL FILES

Format

```
SELECT [OPTIONAL] file-name
    ASSIGN TO implementor-name ...
   [RESERVE integer {AREA | AREAS}]
    [ORGANIZATION IS SEQUENTIAL]
    [ACCESS MODE IS SEQUENTIAL]
    [FILE STATUS IS data-name]
```

Rules

1. file-name is the name of the COBOL file which must be later defined in an FD entry.
2. implementor-name varies in its meaning from implementation to implementation. It is used to link the file-name to the operating system.
3. integer must be greater than zero.
4. data-name must identify a two character alphanumeric data item. It must not be defined in the File Section. It may be qualified.

Function and Effect

The SELECT entry names a file and provides at least part of the link between it and the operating system.

If RESERVE is specified, then integer areas are provided for processing blocks of data read from or written to the file.

ORGANIZATION IS SEQUENTIAL indicates that the data records on the file are organised in such a way that they can only be read in the same sequence as they were written.

ACCESS SEQUENTIAL indicates that the records on the file will be processed in sequence.

FILE STATUS specifies that information about the success or failure of an operation on the file is to be provided in data-name. See FILE STATUS, section 3.11.

If OPTIONAL is specified and the file is not present when an attempt is made to OPEN then the AT END branch will be taken in the first READ statement executed.

Defaults

1. The number of areas reserved if the RESERVE clause is not specified is implementation-defined.
2. If ORGANIZATION is not specified, then SEQUENTIAL is assumed.
3. If ACCESS is not specified, then SEQUENTIAL is assumed.

3.10 SELECT ENTRY – SORT/MERGE FILES

Format

SELECT file-name

    ASSIGN TO implementor-name ...

Rules

1. file-name is the name of a Sort or Merge file which must be later defined in an SD entry.
2. implementor-name varies in meaning from implementation to implementation. It is used to link the file name to the operating system.

Function and Effect

The SELECT entry names a file and provides at least part of the link between it and the operating system.

3.11 FILE STATUS

The data item specified in the FILE STATUS clause of the SELECT entry is a two character data item in which are placed 2 values on execution of an Input/Output operation. Standard values are as follows:

First Character

"0" Successful completion

"1" AT END condition

"2" INVALID KEY condition (doesn't apply to Sequential I/O)

"3" Permanent I/O error

"9" Implementor-defined clause.

Second Character (when first is "2")

"1" Sequence error (Indexed only)

"2" Duplicate key

"3" No record found

"4" Boundary violation.

Many versions of COBOL use additional values and define more precisely the meaning of these standard values.

4 Data Division

4.1 STRUCTURE

Format

```
DATA DIVISION.
[FILE SECTION.
    file description entries, sort description entries and record descriptions]
[WORKING-STORAGE SECTION.
    record descriptions                                                         ]
[LINKAGE SECTION
    record descriptions]
```

Rules and Effects

1. The FILE SECTION is required if and only if the File-Control paragraph was used to define files to be used by the program. The FILE SECTION must contain a file or sort description entry for each file used in the program. Each file and sort description is followed by one description for each different type of record on the file. Only one record area is reserved in central store to be used by all the records read or written regardless of their record descriptions.

2. The WORKING–STORAGE SECTION is required if any data items are to be used which cannot be defined in the FILE or LINKAGE sections.

3. The LINKAGE SECTION is required if the COBOL program in question is to be called from another COBOL program and the Procedure Division heading contains the Using phrase. Every data item specified in the Using phrase must be described in the Linkage Section. No storage is allocated for data items in this section. They use the same storage as the corresponding data items in the calling program.

4.2 FILE DESCRIPTION ENTRY

Format

```
FD file-name

 [BLOCK CONTAINS [integer-1 TO] integer-2 {RECORDS   }]
 [                                        {CHARACTERS}]
 [RECORD CONTAINS [integer-3 TO] integer-4 CHARACTERS ]
 [LABEL {RECORD IS  } {STANDARD}
        {RECORDS ARE} {OMITTED }

 [VALUE OF {implementor-name IS {literal    }} ...]
 [                              {data-name-1}     ]
 [DATA {RECORD IS  }    data-name-2 ...]
 [     {RECORDS ARE}                   ]
 [LINAGE clause]
```

Rules

1. file-name is the name of the COBOL file and must previously have been defined in a SELECT entry.
2. integer-1 to integer-4 must all be unsigned integer values greater than zero.
3. integer-1, if specified, must be less than integer-2.
4. integer-3, if specified, must be less than integer-4.
5. Each data-name-2 is the name of a record following the FD entry.
6. The format of the LINAGE clause follows in section 4.3.

Function and Effect

This entry describes the characteristics of a file.

The BLOCK clause specifies how many characters or logical records are contained in a block of data on the file. If integer-2 only is specified, then the blocks are of fixed length, if integer-1 is also specified, then it and integer-2 specify the minimum and maximum block size respectively. If this clause is omitted, 1 record per block is assumed.

The RECORD CONTAINS clause specifies the size, in characters, of a logical record on the file. If integer-4 only is specified, then the records are fixed in length. If integer-3 also is specified, then it and integer-4 indicate the minimum and maximum record sizes respectively. Since the compiler can calculate the record sizes from the record descriptions, this clause is never required.

The LABEL clause is used to indicate whether or not standard labels are used with the file. The way in which this clause is used varies from one implementation to another. RECORD IS and RECORDS ARE mean exactly the same.

The VALUE OF clause is used sometimes as an extension of the SELECT, to give further identification of the file. Its precise use varies from one implementation to another.

The DATA RECORDS clause shows which records in the program are associated with this file. This serves only as documentation as the records must always follow the FD entry.

The LINAGE clause is used only for files which are destined to be output to a printer. See below for full description.

4.3 LINAGE CLAUSE

Format

```
LINAGE IS { data-name-1 } LINES
          { integer-1   }

    [WITH FOOTING AT { data-name-2 }]
    [                { integer-2   }]

    [LINES AT TOP    { data-name-3 }]
    [                { integer-3   }]

    [LINES AT BOTTOM { data-name-4 }]
    [                { integer-4   }]
```

Rules

1. data-name-1, data-name-2, data-name-3, data-name-4 must refer to unsigned numeric integer data items.
2. The integers, if specified, must follow the rules:

   $0 < \text{integer-2} \leqslant \text{integer-1}$

   $0 \leqslant \text{integer-3}$

   $0 \leqslant \text{integer-4}$

Function and Effect

The clause describes to COBOL the logical characteristics of the printed page associated with the file. data-name-1 (or integer-1) indicates the size in lines of the part of the page in which printing will occur. This part of the page is called the page body. data-name-2 (or integer-2) indicates the starting position, within the page body, of an area known as the footing area. data-name-3 (or integer-3) indicates the number of lines on the logical page before the first line of the page body. data-name-4 (or integer-4) indicates the number of lines on the logical page after the last line of the page body. Thus we have:

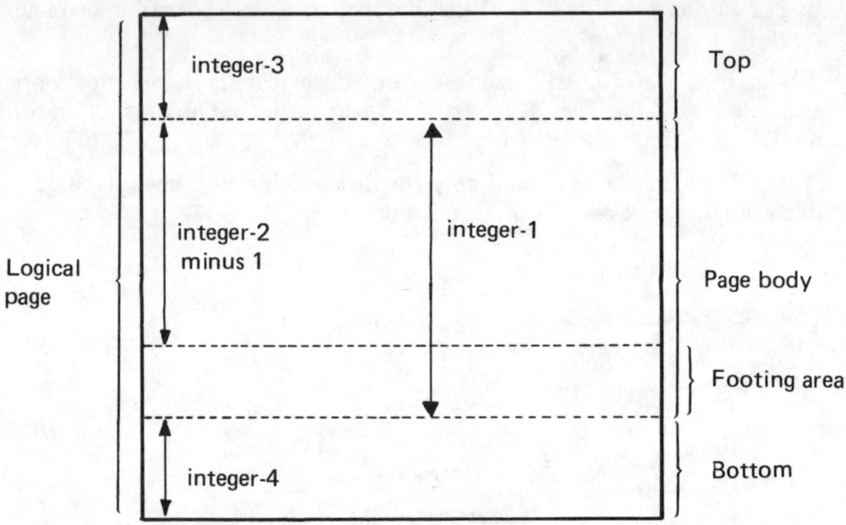

Integer-1, etc above represent the integers specified in the LINAGE clause or the current contents of the corresponding data-name. Where data-names are specified the appropriate data items are inspected when the file is opened, to determine the sizes for the first page, and then each time a new page is reached, to determine the sizes to apply to the second and subsequent pages of the file.

For details of page overflow see section 5.41 – the WRITE statement for printer files.

Defaults

If TOP or BOTTOM are not specified, a value of 0 is assumed.

If FOOTING is not specified, it is assumed to be equal to data-name-1 (or integer-1).

Special Register LINAGE–COUNTER

For every file with the LINAGE clause, COBOL automatically defines a data item called LINAGE–COUNTER. (This needs to be qualified by the file name if more than one LINAGE clause is used in a program).

Procedure Division statements may access the value in LINAGE–COUNTER but may not modify it. The value of LINAGE–COUNTER is set as follows:

On opening the file it is set to 1.

On each WRITE without ADVANCING it is incremented by 1.

On each WRITE with ADVANCING integer or data-name it is incremented by integer or the contents of data-name.

On each WRITE with ADVANCING PAGE it is set to 1.

On each repositioning to a new page it is set to 1.

4.4 SORT–MERGE FILE DESCRIPTION ENTRY

Format

```
SD file-name
  [RECORD CONTAINS integer-1 [TO integer-2] CHARACTERS]
  [DATA {RECORD IS   } data-name ...]
  [     {RECORDS ARE }              ]
```

Rules

1. file-name must previously have been defined in a SELECT entry.
2. integer-1 and integer-2 must be positive integer literals. If both are given then integer-2 must be larger than integer-1.
3. Each data-name is the name of a record following the SD entry.

Function and Effect

The SD entry defines a "file" which the Sort or Merge verb will process. It does not necessarily exist as a file, the source and destination of the data to be sorted being defined by the Sort or Merge verb, and *no* operations may be performed upon file-name except Sort or Merge.

At least one record must be defined in order that the description of the keys and their position within the record can be specified.

Note

The rules and function of the RECORD CONTAINS and DATA RECORDS clauses are described under the File Description entry (section 4.2).

4.5 RECORD DESCRIPTION

Format

data-description-entry-1

[data-description-entry-2] ...

Rules

1. Data-description-entry-1 must contain level number 1.
2. Each data-description-entry-2 must contain a level number in the range 2 to 49 (or level 88 – see below).

4.6 DATA DESCRIPTION ENTRY

Format 1

level-number { data-name | FILLER }

[REDEFINES clause]

[PICTURE clause]

[USAGE clause]

[SIGN clause]

[OCCURS clause]

[SYNCHRONIZED clause]

[JUSTIFIED clause]

[BLANK WHEN ZERO clause]

[VALUE clause (for data items)]

Format 2

88 condition-name VALUE clause (for condition-names)

Rules

1. Level numbers 1 to 9 may be written 01, 02, etc.
2. data-name must follow the rules for forming user-defined names.
3. FILLER data items may not be referenced.
4. Level number 1 must appear in area-A of the coding form, other level numbers may appear in any positions in area-A and B. Everything else in

the data description entry must appear in area-B.

5. The details of the clauses appear in alphabetical order below.

4.7 BLANK WHEN ZERO CLAUSE

Format

BLANK WHEN ZERO

Rules

1. The data item must be numeric or numeric edited. If its picture would otherwise make it numeric, this clause makes it numeric edited.
2. This clause cannot be used when an asterisk is used in the PICTURE clause.

Function and Effect

If this clause is specified, then the data item will be filled with spaces if a value of zero is moved to it. If it receives a value other than zero, this clause has no effect.

4.8 JUSTIFIED CLAUSE

Format

{JUSTIFIED | JUST} RIGHT

Rule

This clause may only be specified for elementary alphanumeric or alphabetic data items.

Function and Effect

This clause has effect when the data item described by it is used as a receiving item. The rightmost character of the data being moved in is aligned with the rightmost character of the receiving item. Any truncation or space filling occurs on the left.

4.9 OCCURS CLAUSE

Format

```
OCCURS integer TIMES
  [ { ASCENDING  }  KEY IS data-name-1 ... ] ...
  [ { DESCENDING }                         ]
  [ INDEXED BY index-name... ]
```

Rules

1. integer must be an unsigned numeric literal.
2. Each data-name-1 must identify a data item subordinate to the entry possessing this clause, or, in the case when only one data-name-1 is specified it may be the data item containing the OCCURS clause. No data-name-1 may be described by an OCCURS clause or be subordinate to an OCCURS clause which is itself subordinate to this clause.
3. Each index name must be a unique name constructed according to the rules for COBOL data-names. They must not be defined elsewhere in the program.
4. OCCURS may not be specified for a data item whose level number is 1 or 88.
5. The VALUE clause may not be specified for an item which has an OCCURS clause or is subordinate to an item with the OCCURS clause (except for format 2 of VALUE used with level 88 items).
6. The data-name having the OCCURS clause, and any subordinate to it, must always be subscripted or indexed when referenced from the Procedure Division with the exception of SEARCH.

Function and Effect

If a data-name has the OCCURS clause, then the data item in question is repeated the number of times specified by integer. If the data item is a group item, then the complete group, including all elementary items, is repeated.

If ASCENDING or DESCENDING are specified, then the data items indicated are keys to the table, the first (leftmost) one being the most significant and last (rightmost) the least significant. (See also Format 2 SEARCH.)

The INDEXED option is used to define index-names.

4.10 OCCURS DEPENDING CLAUSE

Format

OCCURS integer-1 TO integer-2 TIMES DEPENDING ON data-name-2

$$\left[\left\{\begin{array}{l}\underline{\text{ASCENDING}}\\ \underline{\text{DESCENDING}}\end{array}\right\} \text{KEY IS data-name-1} \ldots\right] \ldots$$

[INDEXED BY index-name ...]

Rules

1. integer-1 and integer-2 must be positive integer numeric literals, integer-2 must be larger than integer-1.
2. data-name-2 must identify a numeric data item whose value is a positive integer.
3. data-name-2 may not be subordinate to a data item containing an OCCURS clause.
4. This format of the OCCURS clause may not be specified for a data item subordinate to another item with an OCCURS clause.
5. When a record contains an item with this format of the OCCURS clause then that item, or its last elementary item if it is a group item, must be the last item defined in the record.
6. Rules 2 to 6 in Section 4.9 apply.

Function and Effect

This form of the OCCURS clause defines a table where the number of occurrences is variable. Note that each table item will be fixed in size. The maximum and minimum number of occurrences are given by integer-2 and integer-1 respectively. Whenever reference is made to the table, its current number of occurrences is given by the value of the data-name-2 which must always be in the range integer-1 to integer-2 inclusive.

4.11 PICTURE CLAUSE

Format

$$\left\{\begin{array}{l}\underline{\text{PICTURE}}\\ \underline{\text{PIC}}\end{array}\right\} \text{IS picture-string}$$

Rules

1. A PICTURE clause can only be specified at the elementary level and one must be specified for all elementary items except those described as

USAGE INDEX.

2. The maximum number of characters allowed in picture-string is 30.
3. PIC is an abbreviation for PICTURE.
4. When a string of identical characters appears in picture-string it can be represented by one of the characters followed in brackets by the number of consecutive occurrences of the character.
5. The data item can be classified according to the characters used in picture-string into 5 categories: alphabetic, numeric, numeric edited, alphanumeric and alphanumeric edited.

Each data item belongs to the first category that it matches in the table below.

Category	Permitted Characters in Picture-string
Alphabetic	A B
Numeric	9 V S P
Numeric Edited	9 V P O B / Z * + – , . CR DB £
Alphanumeric	A X 9
Alphanumeric Edited	A X 9 B O /

Note that all group items (including those consisting entirely of numeric items) are of category alphanumeric.

Each category is now discussed in turn.

4.12 ALPHABETIC DATA

Each A represents a letter of the alphabet or a space.

The character B will cause space to appear at the indicated position in the data item whenever a value is moved to the data item.

4.13 NUMERIC DATA

Rules

1. There may be a total of between 1 and 18 occurrences of 9 and P.
2. Each 9 represents one digit.
3. P or a string of Ps can appear only to the left *or* right of the picture-string.

Its presence makes the use of V redundant.

4. There may be 0 or 1 occurrence of V.
5. There may be 0 or 1 occurrence of S, and if present, it must be the first character.

Function and Effect

A data item with a numeric picture may be used for arithmetic processing. If an S is present in the picture, then the data item contains an operational sign, and may be positive, zero or negative. Without an S, the picture indicates an unsigned arithmetic value assumed to be positive if non-zero. The V indicates the assumed position of the decimal point relative to the digits.

If no V is present and no Ps are present, the decimal point is assumed to occur to the right of all the 9s.

If P is present, it specifies the location of an assumed decimal point when the point is not within the number that appears in the data item. Each P on the left of picture-string indicates that the assumed decimal point is moved one position to the left starting to the left of the first 9. Similarly each P on the right of picture-string indicates that the assumed decimal point is moved one position to the right starting to the right of the last 9.

For details of the storage of S see SIGN clause (section 4.18).

4.14 NUMERIC EDITED DATA

1. The following restrictions apply to the Picture characters.

Character	may be followed by:
P	P B O / , + – CR DB 9 V
B	P B O / , . + – CR DB 9 V
O	P B O / , . + – CR DB 9 V
/	P B O / , . + – CR DB 9 V
,	P B O / , . + – CR DB 9 V
.	B O / , + – CR DB 9
+	P B O / , . + £ 9 V
–	P B O / , . – £ 9 V
CR / DB	nothing at all
£	P B O / , . + – CR DB £ 9 V
9	P B O / , . + – CR DB 9 V
V	B O / , + – CR DB 9

Z, * and Floating + and – are discussed below.

2. A single + or – must be the first or last character in the picture-string.
3. Note that there may be only a single . or V in the picture, and not both.
4. Note that P and . cannot both occur in the same picture.
5. In a picture described according to the above rules, one or more occurrences of 9 may be replaced by Z or * subject to:
   a. No 9 character may precede a Z or *.
   b. Z and * may not occur in the same picture.
   c. Digits to the right of V or . must be represented by all 9s, all Zs or all *s.

Zero Suppression

When a value is moved to an edited numeric item containing zero suppression characters (Z or *) then the following may be considered to occur:

1. If the value is zero and there are Zs to the right of the decimal point, then the complete data item is set to blank.
2. If the value is zero and there are *s to the right of the decimal point, then the complete data item is filled with *s, except in a position with a decimal point character where there will be a decimal point.
3. If the value is not zero, then any Z or * characters to the right of the decimal point behave as 9 characters. The value is moved in as if 9s had been used instead of Z or *. Then all character positions containing zeros or simple insertion characters (B O , /) which are to the left of the first significant digit *and* the decimal point receive the zero suppression character (space for Z or asterisk for *) specified for that position.

Simple Insertion Characters

When data is moved into an item with simple insertion characters (B O / , or .) in its picture-string the indicated character (space zero / , or . respectively) is moved into the position represented by the character with the exception indicated above with zero suppression. If the decimal point is present it is aligned with the decimal point of the incoming data (thus it fulfils the function of V as well as being an insertion character).

Sign Characters

When data is moved into an item with a single sign character (+ – CR or DB) in its picture-string the indicated character position will contain the following value:

Sign Character	Data Item Positive or Zero	Data Item Negative
+	+	–
–	space	–
CR	2 spaces	CR
DB	2 spaces	DB

Floating Insertion

Floating insertion occurs when there are two or more £ , – or + characters. The rules are the same as if Zs were used in place of the floating insertion characters except that:

1. the first floating insertion character position may never contain a digit.
2. the rightmost space created by zero suppression is replaced by £ if floating £ used. Alternatively it is replaced by + – or space in accordance with the above table.

Numeric Characters

For Numeric Characters (9 V and P) see Numeric Data.

4.15 ALPHANUMERIC DATA

Each X represents any character in the computer character set.

For A, see Alphabetic Data.

For 9, see Numeric Data.

4.16 ALPHANUMERIC EDITED DATA

The effect of the permitted picture characters (X A 9 B O and /) is as described in the preceding sections.

4.17 REDEFINES CLAUSE

Format

<u>REDEFINES</u> data-name-2

Rules

1. This clause, when used, must be the first coded after the data-name being described.

In the following, data-name-1 refers to the data item to which the REDEFINES clause has been applied.

2. data-name-2 must have the same level number as data-name-1. This level number must not be 01 in the file section, or 88 anywhere.
3. All data items defined between data-name-1 and data-name-2 must have level numbers greater than that of data-name-1, except that it is permitted for one or more data items to be defined having the same level number as long as they also have the REDEFINES clause referencing the same data-name-2.
4. data-name-2 must not have the REDEFINES clause, but may be subordinate to an item with the REDEFINES clause.
5. The amount of storage allocated for data-name-1 must be the same as that allocated for data-name-2.

Function and Effect

A data item with REDEFINES is not allocated new storage of its own, but shares the storage allocated to the data item identified by data-name-2.

Records in the file section for the same file are subject to automatic redefinition.

4.18 SIGN CLAUSE

Format

```
                ⎧ LEADING  ⎫
[SIGN IS]       ⎨          ⎬  [SEPARATE CHARACTER]
                ⎩ TRAILING ⎭
```

Rules

1. The data item with this clause must be numeric with an S picture character.
2. The data item must be USAGE DISPLAY.

Function and Effect

This clause specifies the position of the operational sign in a numeric data item.

If SEPARATE is specified, then the sign is to be represented by a + character or a – character. These will either precede (if LEADING is specified) or follow (if TRAILING is specified) all the digits in the value.

If SEPARATE is not specified, then the sign indication in the value is combined with the first (LEADING) or last (TRAILING) digit position. The way of combining a sign and a digit in a single character will vary from machine to machine.

If SEPARATE is specified the S occupies one character position in the length of the data item. Without SEPARATE the S does not count as a character in the length of the data item.

4.19 SYNCHRONIZED CLAUSE

Format

```
{ SYNCHRONIZED }  [ { LEFT  } ]
{ SYNC         }  [ { RIGHT } ]
```

Rules

The clause may only be specified for elementary items.

Function and Effect

The clause aligns the data item on the natural boundaries of the computer memory (eg word boundary), such that the execution of certain operations (eg arithmetic, subscripting) may be more efficiently handled.

SYNC LEFT positions the elementary item to begin at the leftmost character position of the natural boundary in which the item is placed.

SYNC RIGHT positions the elementary item to terminate at the rightmost character position of the natural boundary.

SYNC alone positions the elementary item between natural boundaries as determined by the implementor for the greatest efficiency.

4.20 USAGE CLAUSE

Format

```
             { COMPUTATIONAL }
             { COMP          }
[USAGE IS]   { DISPLAY       }
             { INDEX         }
```

Rules

1. COMP and COMPUTATIONAL are synonymous.
2. COMP may only be specified for numeric data items (see PICTURE clause – section 4.11) or group items containing only such data items.

3. A data item of USAGE INDEX can be referenced only in a SEARCH or SET statement, a relation condition or a USING phrase.
4. A data item of USAGE INDEX may not contain the SYNCHRONIZED, JUSTIFIED, PICTURE, VALUE or BLANK WHEN ZERO clauses.

Function and Effect

USAGE specifies to the compiler the manner in which the contents of the data item being described are to be held in main storage.

DISPLAY indicates that the data is stored as a string of separate characters.

COMP indicates that the data item may be used for computational purposes and may therefore be stored in the computer in the most suitable way for such purposes.

INDEX indicates that the data item is to be used to store the value of indexes. A data item with this clause is known as an *index data item.*

USAGE may be specified for a group item. This is equivalent to specifying that USAGE for all elementary items within that group item. If USAGE is specified at group level, then none of the contained items may have a conflicting USAGE. Note that the appearance of USAGE IS COMP at group level does *not* permit the group name to be treated as a numeric item.

Default

If an elementary item is given no usage explicitly, then it obtains by default USAGE IS DISPLAY.

4.21 VALUE CLAUSE FOR DATA ITEMS

Format

```
VALUE IS literal
-----
```

Rules

1. This VALUE clause may be specified for data items with level numbers in the range 1 – 49 in the WORKING–STORAGE SECTION.
2. The literal specified must be of a form suitable to be moved to the data item:
   a. If the data item is a group item, then literal must be non-numeric (this includes figurative constants) and its length must not exceed that of the group item.
   b. If the data item is alphanumeric, then the same rules apply as for group items.

c. If the data item is numeric, then literal must be ZERO or a numeric literal. If the data item's picture is signed, the literal must be signed. The size of the literal must be such that no non-zero digits are truncated when the value is moved to the data item.

d. If the data item is numeric edited, then the value must be given as a non-numeric literal containing data in the edited form suitable for the data item. No editing takes place when the value is moved in.

3. This VALUE clause may not be specified for any data item which has, or is within a group which has, the OCCURS or REDEFINES clause.
4. This VALUE clause may not be specified for any group item which contains data items with USAGE, VALUE, JUSTIFIED or SYNCHRONIZED clauses (except USAGE IS DISPLAY).

Function and Effect

The specified value is placed in the data item prior to the execution of the program. Note that this is a once-only action: subsequent modification of the contents of a data item (for example by a MOVE statement) destroys the initial value.

4.22 VALUE CLAUSE FOR CONDITION–NAMES

Format

$$\left\{\begin{matrix}\underline{\text{VALUE}}\text{ IS}\\ \underline{\text{VALUES}}\text{ ARE}\end{matrix}\right\}\left\{\text{literal-1}\left[\left\{\begin{matrix}\underline{\text{THROUGH}}\\ \underline{\text{THRU}}\end{matrix}\right\}\text{ literal-2}\right]\right\}\ldots$$

Rules

1. This format of the VALUE clause completes the data description entry which begins 88 condition-name. This entry is associated with the data item (level 1 to 49) which precedes it.
2. VALUE IS and VALUES ARE are synonymous, as are THROUGH and THRU.
3. The form of literal-1 and literal-2 must be suitable for the associated data item (see Section 4.21, rule 2).
4. If the THROUGH clause is specified, literal-2 must be greater than literal-1.

Function and Effect

The VALUE clause for a condition-name serves to define the ranges of values for the associated data item which cause a "true" result to be given by a reference to the condition-name.

The condition-name is true if the associated data item contains the value of any instance of literal-1 or, when THROUGH is specified, any value between literal-1 and literal-2 inclusive.

5 Procedure Division

5.1 STRUCTURE

Formats

1. PROCEDURE DIVISION [USING data-name ...].

   { section-name SECTION.

   { paragraph-name.

   [sentence] ... } ... } ...

2. PROCEDURE DIVISION [USING data-name ...].

   { paragraph-name.

   [sentence] ... } ...

5.2 USING PHRASE IN PROCEDURE DIVISION HEADER

Format

USING data-name ...

Rules

1. data-name must be defined in the LINKAGE SECTION and have a level number of 1.
2. the number of data-names must equal the number of data-names in the USING phrase of any CALL statement used to invoke the program.

Function and Effect

This form of the PROCEDURE DIVISION heading must be used whenever the program is to be called with a CALL statement having the USING phrase. The data-names are used to access the data items specified in the corresponding CALL statement.

5.3 ACCEPT STATEMENT

Format

1. ACCEPT identifier [FROM mnemonic-name]

2. ACCEPT identifier FROM { DAY | DATE | TIME }

Rules

1. In format 1, mnemonic-name must be defined in SPECIAL–NAMES to refer to a particular input device.
2. In format 2, identifier must identify a data item able to receive an unsigned integer value of 8 digits (for TIME), 6 digits (for DATE), or 5 digits (for DAY).

Function and Effect

In format 1, data is transferred left-aligned from the specified device to the data item indicated by identifier. The data input may be shorter than the data item. If the data input is longer, then truncation occurs at the right-hand end. Note that ACCEPT ignores any use of JUSTIFIED in the data description of identifier.

In format 2, the statement moves to identifier the current day, date or time, depending upon whether DAY, DATE or TIME is specified.

DAY behaves as a 5 digit numeric item having as its first 2 digits the year number within century and as its last 3 digits the day number within year.

DATE behaves as a 6 digit numeric item having as its first 2 digits the year number within century, as the next 2 digits the month number within year and as the last 2 digits the day number within year.

TIME behaves as an 8 digit number indicating the time elapsed since the most recent midnight, with its first 2 digits being hours, the next 2 digits minutes, the next 2 digits seconds, and the last 2 digits being hundredths of a second. The accuracy of the last 2 digits will depend upon the hardware being used.

Default

In format 1, if the FROM phrase is omitted, the standard device specified by the implementor is used for the input.

5.4 ADD STATEMENT

Format

```
1. ADD { identifier-1 } ...  TO { identifier-2 [ROUNDED] } ...
       { literal-1    }

       [ON SIZE ERROR imperative-statement]

2. ADD { identifier-1 } { identifier-2 } ...
       { literal-1    } { literal-2    }

       GIVING { identifier-3 [ROUNDED] } ...

       [ON SIZE ERROR imperative-statement]
```

For ADD CORRESPONDING see CORRESPONDING option (section 6.6).

Rules

1. literal-1 and literal-2 must be numeric literals.
2. identifier-1 and identifier-2 must reference numeric data items.
3. identifier-3 must reference either a numeric data item or a numeric edited data item.

Function and Effect

The ADD statement adds together specified numeric values and places the result in a specified data item or items. The two formats operate differently, and so will be considered separately.

In format 1 the values of all identifiers and/or literals between ADD and TO are added. The resulting value is then *added* in turn to each of the identifiers following TO.

In format 2 the values of all identifiers and/or literals between ADD and GIVING are added. The resulting value is then *moved* in turn to each of the identifiers following GIVING.

For the effect of ROUNDED, see section 6.14.

For the effect of ON SIZE ERROR, see section 6.15.

5.5 CALL STATEMENT

Format

```
CALL {"program-name"} [USING data-name ...]
     {identifier    }

    [ON OVERFLOW imperative-statement]
```

Rules

1. identifier must be an alphanumeric data item.
2. data-name must identify a data item with level number 1.

Function and Effect

Control passes to the program identified by the literal or the contents of the identifier. When that 'called' program terminates, then control returns to the statement following the CALL statement. The called program must terminate by executing an EXIT PROGRAM statement. If the USING phrase is specified, then the data items specified are made available to the called program *in the order specified.* They will be accessed through corresponding data items specified in the USING phrase of the PROCEDURE DIVISION header and defined in the called program's LINKAGE SECTION.

Note that recursion is not allowed, ie a program may not be called while it is already being executed.

imperative-statement is executed if there is insufficient main storage available for the execution of the called program. If this situation arises and OVERFLOW was not specified then the results are not defined.

5.6 CANCEL STATEMENT

Format

```
CANCEL {"program-name"} ...
       {identifier    }
```

Rules

1. identifier must be an alphanumeric data item.
2. The program identified by the literal or the contents of the identifier must not be in a partially executed state.

Function and Effect

The storage space occupied by each program specified is freed and if the program is CALLed again it will have been returned to its initial state (the VALUE clauses will have been re-applied, etc).

5.7 CLOSE STATEMENT

Format

CLOSE file-name ...

Rules

1. All file-names must be the names of files which are open when the CLOSE statement is executed.
2. All open files must be closed via a CLOSE statement prior to program termination.

Function and Effect

The COBOL file is dissociated from the file of data. If the file was opened for OUTPUT or EXTEND then any end markers are written on the file. After the execution of CLOSE the record areas for the closed files are no longer available.

5.8 COMPUTE STATEMENT

Format

COMPUTE { identifier [ROUNDED] } ... = arithmetic-expression

[ON SIZE ERROR imperative-statement]

Rules

identifier must be a numeric or numeric edited data item.

Function and Effect

The COMPUTE statement evaluates an arithmetic expression and places the result in identifier. Note that the evaluation of the expression occurs once only, thus if one of the identifiers occurs within the expression, the new value it receives during execution of the statement is *not* used in the calculation of the value to be moved to subsequent identifiers.

For the effect of ROUNDED, see section 6.14.

For the effect of ON SIZE ERROR, see section 6.15.

5.9 DELETE STATEMENT – INDEXED FILES

Format

```
DELETE file-name RECORD
       [INVALID KEY imperative-statement]
```

Rules

1. file-name must have ORGANIZATION INDEXED and be opened for I–O.
2. the INVALID KEY phrase must not be specified for sequential access files.
3. for random and dynamic access files the INVALID KEY phrase must be specified.

Function and Effect

This statement deletes from the specified file the record whose key is equal to the value of the data item specified in the RECORD KEY clause.

In sequential access mode, the record deleted is the last one read. The last operation on the file must have been a successful READ.

In random or dynamic access mode, the record deleted is the one identified by the value in the RECORD KEY data item. If this does not identify a record then imperative-statement will be executed.

5.10 DELETE STATEMENT – RELATIVE FILES

Format

```
DELETE file-name RECORD
       [INVALID KEY imperative-statement]
```

Rules

1. file-name must have ORGANIZATION RELATIVE and be opened for I–O.
2. The INVALID KEY phrase must not be specified for sequential access files.
3. The INVALID KEY phrase must be specified for random and dynamic access files.

Function and Effect

This statement deletes the record from the file specified by file-name.

In sequential access mode, the record deleted is the last one read. The last operation on the file must have been a successful READ.

In random or dynamic access mode, the record deleted is the one identified by the value in the RELATIVE KEY data item. If this does not identify a record, then imperative-statement will be executed.

5.11 DISPLAY STATEMENT

Format

```
          { identifier }
DISPLAY   {            } ... [UPON mnemonic-name]
          { literal    }
```

Rules

1. literal may be any non-numeric or unsigned integer numeric literal, or any figurative constant except ALL.
2. mnemonic-name must have been defined as a specific hardware device in the SPECIAL–NAMES paragraph in the ENVIRONMENT DIVISION.

Function and Effect

The DISPLAY statement transfers the data items listed to an output peripheral.

A "sending item" is created from the concatenation of all the items specified. Intervening spaces are *not* automatically inserted, and each use of a figurative constant produces a single occurrence of that character. If the "sending item" exceeds the line size of the peripheral then the "sending item" is split over more than one line. If the line size exceeds the length of the "sending item" then the "sending item" is extended on the right with spaces.

Default

If the UPON phrase is not specified, then the output is performed on the implementor's standard low-volume output device.

5.12 DIVIDE STATEMENT

Formats

```
1.        { identifier-1 }
   DIVIDE {              }   INTO { identifier-2 [ROUNDED] } ...
          { literal-1    }

      [ON SIZE ERROR imperative-statement]

2.        { identifier-1 } { INTO } { identifier-2 }
   DIVIDE {              } {      } {              }
          { literal-1    } { BY   } { literal-2    }

      GIVING { identifier-3 [ROUNDED] } ...
      [REMAINDER identifier-4]
      [ON SIZE ERROR imperative-statement]
```

Rules

1. literal-1 and literal-2 must be numeric literals.
2. identifier-1 and identifier-2 must be numeric data items.
3. identifier-3 and identifier-4 may be numeric data items or numeric edited data items.
4. In format 2, if REMAINDER is specified then only a single identifier-3 may be given.

Function and Effect

In format 1 each identifier-2 in turn has its value divided by identifier-1 or literal-1, identifier-1 remains unchanged.

In format 2 if INTO is specified the result is obtained by dividing identifier-2 or literal-2 by identifier-1 or literal-1. If BY is specified the result is obtained by dividing identifier-1 or literal-1 by identifier-2 or literal-2. The result is moved to each identifier-3 (following normal rules for MOVE).

If the REMAINDER phrase is specified a remainder is calculated as follows:

a. If INTO is specified the value in identifier-3 is multiplied by identifier-1 or literal-1 and the result is subtracted from identifier-2 or literal-2.
b. If BY is specified the value in identifier-3 is multiplied by identifier-2 or literal-2 and the result is subtracted from identifier-1 or literal-1.

The remainder thus calculated is moved into identifier-4.

Note that the *unrounded* (ie truncated) result of the division is used to calculate the remainder. If ROUNDED is specified the rounding is done after the calculation of the remainder.

For the effect of ROUNDED, see section 6.14.

For the effect of ON SIZE ERROR, see section 6.15.

5.13 EXIT STATEMENT

Format

<u>EXIT</u>

Rules

The EXIT statement must be the only statement in the only sentence in a paragraph.

Function and Effect

The EXIT statement is purely documentary. Its most common use is to mark the exit point of a PERFORMed routine.

5.14 EXIT PROGRAM STATEMENT

Format

EXIT PROGRAM

Rules

This must be the only statement in the only sentence in a paragraph.

Function and Effect

This statement returns control from a called program to the point whence it was called. If the program in which the EXIT PROGRAM statement appears was not invoked with a CALL statement then the statement has no effect.

5.15 GO TO STATEMENT

Format

GO TO procedure-name

Rules

procedure-name must be the name of a paragraph or section in the Procedure Division.

Function and Effect

The GO TO statement causes control to pass to the first statement in the specified paragraph or section.

5.16 GO TO ... DEPENDING STATEMENT

Format

GO TO procedure-name-1 procedure-name-2 ... DEPENDING ON identifier

Rules

1. procedure-name-1 and procedure-name-2 must be the names of paragraphs or sections in the Procedure Division.
2. identifier must identify a numeric integer data item.

Function and Effect

This version of the GO TO statement passes control to one of several points in the program, controlled by the value in identifier. When the statement is executed, if identifier has a value less than 1 or greater than the number of procedure-names specified, control passes to the next statement. Otherwise control passes to the procedure-name whose position in the list is the same as the value in identifier.

5.17 IF STATEMENT

Format

```
IF condition { statement-1      } [ ELSE statement-2       ]
             { NEXT SENTENCE    } [ ELSE NEXT SENTENCE     ]
```

Rules

1. condition may be any COBOL condition (See section 6.4).
2. statement-1 and statement-2 may be imperative or conditional statements. If either of them contains an IF statement, then the construct is described as a nested IF (see below).
3. ELSE NEXT SENTENCE may be omitted if it immediately precedes the terminating period of the sentence.

Function and Effect

The IF statement provides a choice of two statements to be executed depending upon the truth or otherwise of the specified condition.

Thus

If the condition is true and statement-1 is specified, then statement-1 is executed and control passes to the next sentence.

If the condition is true and statement-1 is not specified, then control passes directly to the next sentence.

If the condition is false and statement-2 is specified, then statement-2 is executed and control passes to the next sentence.

If the condition is false and statement-2 is not specified, then control passes directly to the next sentence.

Note that in the above discussion, if statement-1 or statement-2 contain a statement (a GO TO statement, for example) which passes control out of the IF statement, then control continues as normal. If, however, a PERFORM or CALL statement which returns normally is executed within statement-1 or statement-2, then upon return of control the IF will continue as described above.

Nested IFs

If statement-1 contains an IF statement, then the structure is complicated by the fact that there may be two ELSEs with no intervening IF. First each ELSE must be matched with its corresponding IF: sequentially from left to right each ELSE is paired with the IF nearest to it on its left which has not already been paired with an ELSE. This procedure is followed no matter to what depth the IFs may be nested.

Thus for nested IFs, the extent of statement-1 is from the end of the condition up to the *corresponding* ELSE or the end of the sentence (whichever comes first).

5.18 INSPECT STATEMENT

Format

```
INSPECT identifier-1
   [TALLYING { identifier-2 FOR { tally-spec [limit-spec] } ... } ...]

                  { { ALL     }                                                 }
   [REPLACING     { { LEADING } {string-replace-spec [limit-spec] }... }...     }]
                  { { FIRST   }                                                 }
                  {                                                             }
                  {  characters-replace-spec [limit-spec]                       }
```

where tally-spec is

```
{ { ALL     }      { identifier-3 } }
{ { LEADING }      { literal-3    } }
{ CHARACTERS                        }
```

limit-spec is

```
{ BEFORE }           { identifier-4 }
{ AFTER  } INITIAL   { literal-4    }
```

string-replace-spec is

```
{ identifier-5 }  BY  { identifier-6 }
{ literal-5    }      { literal-6    }
```

and characters-replace-spec is

```
CHARACTERS BY { identifier-6 }
              { literal-6    }
```

Rules

1. identifier-1 must reference a USAGE IS DISPLAY data item.
2. identifier-2 must reference a numeric data item.
3. identifier-3, identifier-4, identifier-5 and identifier-6 must reference elementary items of USAGE DISPLAY.

4. Each literal may be non-numeric or any figurative constant except ALL.
5. If literal-3 or literal-4 are figurative constants they are of one character length.
6. When identifier-5 or literal-5 is specified the size of data represented by identifier-6 or literal-6 must equal the size of data represented by identifier-5 or literal-5. If literal-6 is a figurative constant its size is taken to be the same as identifier-5 or literal-5 (whichever is specified).
7. When the CHARACTERS phrase is used the size of data represented by identifier-6, identifier-7, literal-6 and literal-7 must be one character.
8. When literal-5 is a figurative constant the size of data represented by identifier-6 or literal-6 must be one character.
9. At least one TALLYING or REPLACING phrase must be specified.

Function and Effect

INSPECT scans the contents of identifier-1 counting and/or replacing characters under the control of the TALLYING and REPLACING phrases respectively.

All TALLYING phrases are processed before any REPLACING phrases.

Function of the limit-spec:

Each TALLYING or REPLACING specification may be qualified by a limit-spec. Without a limit-spec the phrase is considered to apply to the whole of the identifier-1. With limit-spec the part of identifier-1 to be acted upon by the phrase is:

a. If BEFORE specified,
   that part of identifier-1 to the left of the leftmost occurrence of the delimiter (the contents of identifier-4 or literal-4).
b. If AFTER specified,
   that part of identifier-1 to the right of the leftmost occurrence of the delimiter.

If the delimiter is not present within identifier-1, then BEFORE implies the whole string and AFTER implies no characters at all.

Note that the starting/stopping points of each tally-spec or replace-spec are determined before any tallying or replacing.

Overall Action of the Statement

1. Executing the TALLYING phrases.

With CHARACTERS, identifier-2 is incremented by the number of characters in that part of identifier-1 being acted on (see the paragraph on limit-spec above).

With ALL, identifier-2 is incremented by the number of complete occurrences of the contents of identifier-3 or literal-3 present in that part of identifier-1 being acted on.

With LEADING, identifier-2 is incremented by the number of complete occurrences of the contents of identifier-3 or literal-3 to the left of any other characters in that part of identifier-1 being acted on.

2. Executing the REPLACING phrases

   a. CHARACTERS specified.

      Every character in that part of identifier-1 being acted on is replaced by literal-6 or the contents of identifier-6.

   b. CHARACTERS not specified.

      We will use X to refer to the leftmost character in identifier-1 which has not yet been processed by a REPLACING phrase. Initially this will be the leftmost character of identifier-1. Each of the string-replace-specs in turn is tested for a 'match'. This occurs when literal-5 or the contents of identifier-5 is equal to a sub-string of identifier-1 starting at X which falls within the corresponding limit-spec. If no match occurs, X becomes the next character in identifier-1, unless X was the last character in identifier-1 – in which case the INSPECT statement terminates. If a match does occur then:

      ALL

      The characters in identifier-1 equal to literal-5 or the contents of identifier-5 are replaced by literal-6 or the contents of identifier-6.

      FIRST

      If a match with literal-5 or the contents of identifier-5 has already occurred in that part of identifier-1 being acted on by this replace-spec, then this match is considered not to have occurred. Otherwise the characters in identifier-1 equal to literal-5 or the contents of identifier-5 are replaced by literal-6 or the contents of identifier-6.

      LEADING

      If the first match is not at the beginning of that part of identifier-1 being acted on by the replace-spec then no replacement takes place. Otherwise this matching string and all matching strings contiguous to it are replaced by literal-6 or the contents of identifier-6.

As soon as a match occurs, then the replacement for that match is performed. Testing for a match then recommences with the first character after the last character replaced.

5.19 MERGE STATEMENT

Format

```
MERGE file-name-1
    { ON { ASCENDING  } KEY data-name ... } ...
         { DESCENDING }
    USING file-name-2 file-name-3 ...
  { OUTPUT PROCEDURE IS section-name-1 [ { THROUGH } section-name-2 ] }
  {                                      { THRU    }                  }
  { GIVING file-name-4                                                }
```

Rules

1. file-name-1 must be defined in an SD entry in the Data Division.
2. Each data-name must refer to a data item described within a record associated with file-name. It may not have the OCCURS clause nor be subordinate to one. It may not contain an item with the OCCURS clause with the DEPENDING option.
3. If section-name-2 is specified it must appear later in the program than section-name-1.
4. No coding executed from the output procedure may be executed from any other part of the program.
5. file-name-2, file-name-3 and file-name-4 must be defined in FD entries.

Function and Effect

The MERGE statement combines the records from two or more files into a single file maintaining the sequence specified within the statement.

Input to the MERGE

The files specified in the USING phrase must all be closed when the MERGE is executed. The MERGE statement will open the files itself before reading them, and will close them all afterwards. The records for the incoming files must all have the same length as the records defined for file-name. Each of the files must already be sorted into the sequence defined by the ASCENDING/DESCENDING clause.

Output from the MERGE

GIVING

The MERGE writes, to the specified file, the records in the specified sequence. The file is opened and closed automatically by MERGE: it must not be open when the MERGE verb is executed.

OUTPUT PROCEDURE

The specified procedure is invoked when the MERGE reaches a point where it can start outputting the records in merged order. Each time RETURN is executed, a record is passed from the MERGE to the output procedure. Note that the procedure may contain neither SORT nor MERGE statements.

IDENTICAL KEYS

If identical keys exist, then the records are written to the output (GIVING) file, or presented to the output procedure in the order in which the files are specified in the USING phrase.

5.20 MOVE STATEMENT

Format

```
       { identifier-1 }
MOVE   {              }   TO identifier-2 ...
       { literal      }
```

For the use of MOVE CORRESPONDING, see CORRESPONDING option (section 6.6).

Rules

None of the identifiers may be Index names or Index data items.

Function and Effects

The MOVE statement copies the value from the sending item (identifier-1 or literal) to the receiving item(s) (identifier-2...). The sending item remains unchanged, the receiving items all lose their original values and receive the value being moved.

Certain combinations of sending and receiving data types are not permitted. The table below shows the valid (marked Y) and invalid (marked N) combinations.

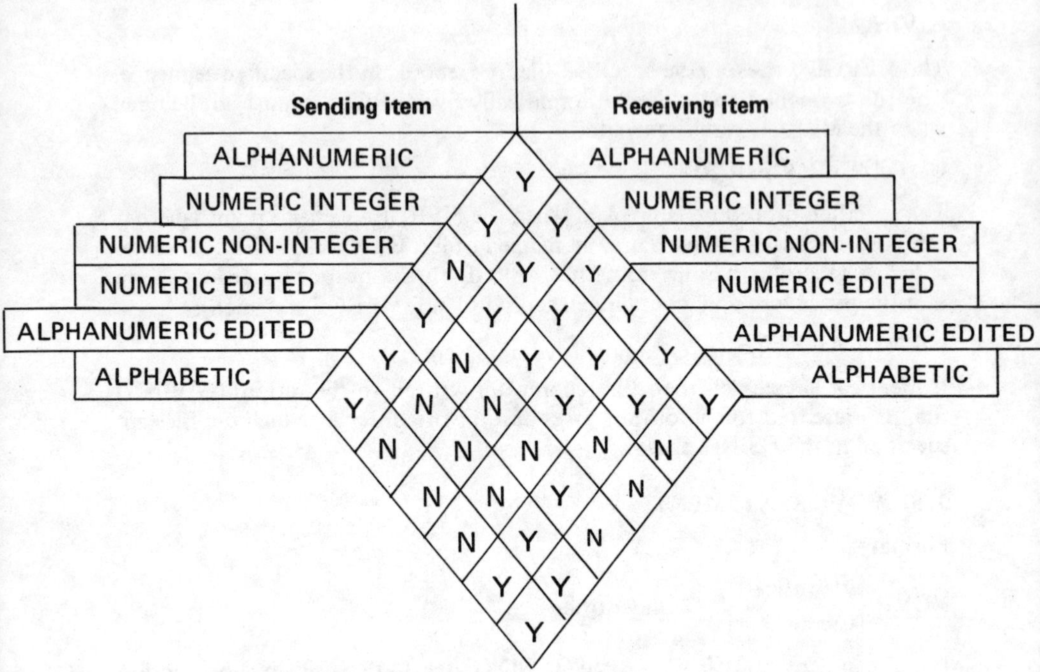

Notes on moves with **numeric** *receiving items.*

1. Alignment is on the decimal point.
2. Excess positions in the receiving item are filled with zeros unless specified, otherwise by editing characters.
3. An alphanumeric item may only be moved to a numeric item when the sending item consists entirely of numeric digits.

Notes on moves with **alphanumeric** *receiving items.*

1. If the receiving item is defined as JUSTIFIED RIGHT the rightmost characters of the sending and receiving items are aligned.
2. If the JUSTIFIED RIGHT clause is omitted the leftmost characters of the sending and receiving items are aligned.
3. Excess positions in the receiving item are space filled.
4. Truncation occurs if the receiving item is not large enough to receive the sending item .

Notes on moves with *alphabetic* receiving items.

1. An alphanumeric item may only be moved to an alphabetic item when the sending item consists entirely of alphabetic characters.
2. Alignment, truncation and space filling rules are the same for alphabetic receiving items as for alphanumeric receiving items.

5.21 MULTIPLY STATEMENT

Format

```
1.  MULTIPLY {identifier-1} BY {identifier-2 [ROUNDED]} ...
             {literal-1   }

        [ON SIZE ERROR imperative-statement]

2.  MULTIPLY {identifier-1} BY {identifier-2}
             {literal-1   }    {literal-2   }

        GIVING {identifier-3 [ROUNDED]} ...

        [ON SIZE ERROR imperative-statement]
```

Rules

1. All literals must be numeric literals.
2. identifier-1 and identifier-2 must be elementary numeric data items.
3. identifier-3 must be a numeric data item or a numeric edited data item.

Function and Effect

The MULTIPLY statement multiplies pairs of numeric values, and places the result in a specified data item. The two formats operate differently and so will be considered separately.

In format 1 identifier-2 has its value multiplied by the value of identifier-1 or literal-1, the resultant value being stored in identifier-2.

In format 2 the value of identifier-1 or literal-1 is multiplied by identifier-2 or literal-2. The result of this operation is moved to identifier-3 (following the normal rules for MOVE).

For the effect of ROUNDED see section 6.14.

For the effect of ON SIZE ERROR see section 6.15.

5.22 OPEN STATEMENT

Format

```
       { INPUT file-name-1...   }
OPEN   { OUTPUT file-name-2...  }  ...
       { I-O file-name-3...     }
       { EXTEND file-name-4...  }
```

Rules

1. As many files as desired can be opened in a single statement; files to be opened for INPUT have their names specified after INPUT, those for OUTPUT after OUTPUT, etc.
2. A file may be opened several times within a program, as long as it is closed when each OPEN statement is executed.
3. All files to be processed must first be opened in an OPEN statement.

Function and Effect

The OPEN statement associates a COBOL file with a file of data. It makes the record area (defined in File Section) available and prepares the file for processing. Any labels associated with the file, as specified in the LABEL RECORDS clause, may also be checked.

When the EXTEND option is used the record pointer (indicating the current position in the file) is set to the position following the last record in the named file(s). Subsequent WRITE statements to the file(s) will add on records in the same way as for files opened as OUTPUT.

OPEN I–O allows both input and output operations on the same file. It cannot be used for file creation.

5.23 PERFORM STATEMENT – PART 1

Formats

1.

```
PERFORM procedure-name-1  [ { THROUGH } procedure-name-2 ]
                          [ { THRU    }                  ]
```

2.

```
PERFORM procedure-name-1  [ { THROUGH } procedure-name-2 ]  { identifier }  TIMES
                          [ { THRU    }                  ]  { literal    }
```

3.

```
PERFORM procedure-name-1  [ { THROUGH } procedure-name-2 ]  UNTIL condition
                          [ { THRU    }                  ]
```

Rules

1. procedure-name-1 and procedure-name-2 may be names of paragraphs or sections in the Procedure Division.
2. identifier must identify an integer numeric data item. literal must be an unsigned numeric integer.
3. condition may be any COBOL condition.

Function and Effect

Format 1

On execution of the PERFORM, control passes to the first statement in procedure-name-1. When control, by any route, reaches the last statement in procedure-name-1, or procedure-name-2 if specified, then control returns to the statement following the PERFORM statement.

Format 2

Has the same effect as format 1 except that the whole process occurs a number of times determined by identifier or literal. If identifier is zero or negative when the PERFORM statement is reached, then control passes immediately to the statement following PERFORM. Note that modification of identifier during the performance of the specified procedure(s) will *not* affect the number of times those procedures are performed.

Format 3

Has the same effect as format 1 except that the whole process is repeated under the control of the truth of condition. Before each performance, including the first, the value of condition is tested. If it is true, then control passes to the statement following PERFORM. If it is not true the specified procedure(s) are performed. The loop thus caused can only be broken by modification of the value of some data item tested within condition.

Notes on the Scopes of Performs

1. A PERFORM statement may not be executed while it is already active, ie recursion is not allowed.
2. Two PERFORMs, active simultaneously, cannot have a common end point.
3. If, during the execution of a PERFORM statement, another PERFORM statement is encountered, then the set of procedures referred to by the second PERFORM must lie either totally outside or totally inside the set referred to by the first PERFORM. This applies also to more deeply nested PERFORMs.

5.24 PERFORM STATEMENT – PART 2

Format 4

```
                            [ { THROUGH }                     ]
PERFORM procedure-name-1    [ { THRU    }  procedure-name-2   ]

        VARYING loop-1

        [AFTER  loop-2 [AFTER loop-3] ]
```

where loop-1, loop-2 and loop-3 are of the form:

```
                          { identifier-2 }
{ identifier-1 }   FROM   { index-name-2 }   BY   { identifier-3 }   UNTIL condition
{ index-name-1 }          { literal-2    }        { literal-3    }
```

Rules

1. procedure-name-1 and procedure-name-2 may be names of paragraphs or sections in the Procedure Division.
2. literal-3 may not be zero.
3. literal-2 and literal-3 must be numeric.
4. Each identifier must represent a numeric data item.
5. If index-name-1 is specified, then identifier-2 and identifier-3 must represent integer data items, literal-2 must be a positive integer and literal-3 must be an integer.
6. If index-name-2 is specified then identifier-1 and identifier-3 must represent integer data items and literal-3 must be an integer.

Function and Effect

For the purpose of the following descriptions identifier-1 or index-name-1 will be referred to as *counter*, literal-2 or the contents of identifier-2 or index-name-2 will be referred to as *start-value*, and literal-3 or the contents of identifier-3 will be referred to as *step-value*.

This format of PERFORM executes the specified procedure(s) zero or more times (depending upon the condition values) while controlling the values of the counter(s) according to the start-value(s) and step-value(s) specified.

Without the use of AFTER, a single counter is stepped from its starting value until the associated condition is satisfied (this is referred to as a *complete loop*).

If loop-2 is specified it executes its complete loop for each value of counter in loop-1.

If loop-3 is specified it executes its complete loop for each value of counter in loop-2.

Action of a Complete Loop

The logic followed for a loop specified with VARYING or AFTER is as follows:

1. Move start-value to counter.
2. Test the condition. If true, then this loop is finished.
3. If the condition is false, PERFORM procedure-name-1 (THRU procedure-name-2). Augment counter by step-value. Return to 2.

5.25 READ STATEMENT – INDEXED FILES

Format

```
1. READ file-name-1 [NEXT] RECORD [INTO identifier]
           AT END imperative-statement
```

used for sequential reading.

```
2. READ file-name-2 RECORD [INTO identifier]
           [KEY IS data-name]
           INVALID KEY imperative-statement
```

used for random reading.

Rules

1. file-name-1 must be a file with ORGANIZATION INDEXED and ACCESS SEQUENTIAL or DYNAMIC, opened for INPUT or I–O. For DYNAMIC, NEXT must be specified.
2. file-name-2 must be a file with ORGANIZATION INDEXED and ACCESS RANDOM or DYNAMIC, opened for INPUT or I–O.
3. The INTO phrase must not be used with variable length record files.
4. identifier must not refer to all or part of the file's record area.
5. data-name must be the name of a data item defined as a key for this file (ie it must appear in a RECORD KEY or ALTERNATE KEY clause in the select entry). It may be qualified.

Function and Effect

This statement transfers the selected record, if available, from the file into the record area for the file (and into identifier if specified).

Which record is the 'selected' record depends upon the format of READ statement used.

With format 1 the selected record is the first in the file (if no reads have been executed since the opening of the file), or the one following the last one read or rewritten, or the first record available from the position in the file set by a Start statement. If a sequential Read reaches the end of the file the AT END statement is executed. In this case the contents of the file's record area are undefined (though identifier, if specified, is unchanged).

With format 2 the selected record is the one identified by KEY IS or RECORD KEY in SELECT (KEY IS having precedence). If the key value specified does not identify any record on the file then the INVALID KEY statement is executed.

5.26 READ STATEMENT – RELATIVE FILES

Format

```
1. READ file-name-1 [NEXT] RECORD [INTO identifier]
       AT END imperative-statement
```

used for sequential reading.

```
2. READ file-name-2 RECORD [INTO identifier]
       INVALID KEY imperative-statement
```

used for random reading.

Rules

1. file-name-1 must be a file with ORGANIZATION RELATIVE and ACCESS SEQUENTIAL or DYNAMIC, opened for INPUT or I–O. For DYNAMIC, NEXT must be specified.
2. file-name-2 must be a file with ORGANIZATION RELATIVE and ACCESS RANDOM or DYNAMIC, opened for INPUT or I–O.
3. The INTO phrase must not be used with variable length record files.
4. identifier must not refer to all or part of the file's record area.

Function and Effect

This statement transfers the selected record, if available, from the file into the record area for the file (and into identifier if specified).

Which record is the 'selected' record depends upon the format of READ statement used.

With format 1 the selected record is the first in the file (if no reads have been executed since the opening of the file), or the one following the last one read, or the first record available from the position in the file set by a Start statement. If a sequential Read reaches the end of the file the AT END statement is executed. In this case the contents of the file's record area are undefined (though identifier if specified is unchanged).

With format 2 the selected record is the one identified by the RELATIVE KEY data-item. If the key value specified does not identify any record on the file, then the INVALID statement is executed.

5.27 READ STATEMENT – SEQUENTIAL FILES

Format

READ file-name RECORD [INTO identifier] AT END imperative-statement

Rules

1. file-name must identify a file currently opened for INPUT or I–O.
2. identifier must not refer to all or part of the file's record area.
3. The INTO phrase must not be used with variable length record files.

Function and Effect

The statement reads the next record in the specified file. The record is always placed in the record area associated with the file. If the INTO phrase is specified then, after the record has been read, COBOL executes a MOVE from the record area to the identifier specified. In this case the data from the record is available in both areas after completion of the READ.

If, when the READ is executed, there is no next record on the file, then imperative-statement is executed.

5.28 RELEASE STATEMENT

Format

RELEASE record-name [FROM identifier]

Rules

1. The RELEASE statement must only be used in the Input Procedure of a SORT statement.
2. record-name must be the name of a record associated with the SD entry referenced by the SORT statement in rule 1.
3. identifier must not share any storage with record-name.

Function and Effect

The RELEASE statement passes a record to the Sort. If FROM is specified, then the statement is equivalent to:

```
MOVE identifier TO record-name.
RELEASE record-name.
```

When control passes from the input procedure, the SORT statement will sort all the records which have been released to it.

5.29 RETURN STATEMENT

Format

```
RETURN file-name RECORD [INTO identifier]
    AT END imperative-statement
```

Rules

1. file-name must appear in an SD entry in the Data division.
2. the RETURN statement must only be coded within the Output Procedure of a SORT or MERGE statement which references file-name.
3. identifier must not be a record or part of a record associated with file-name.
4. the INTO phrase must not be used when variable length records are being processed.

Function and Effect

The RETURN statement is used in a Sort or Merge Output Procedure to request from the Sort or Merge the next record in sequence. If INTO is specified then the statement is equivalent to:

```
RETURN file-name RECORD AT END imperative-statement
MOVE record-name TO identifier.
```

where record-name is the name of a record for file-name.

If no logical record exists for the file at the time of the RETURN statement's execution, imperative-statement is executed and the contents of the file's record area are undefined. After execution of imperative-statement no RETURN statement may be executed as part of the current output procedure.

5.30 REWRITE STATEMENT

Format

```
REWRITE record-name [FROM identifier]
    [INVALID KEY imperative-statement]
```

Rules

1. record-name must be the name of a record associated with a file opened for I–O.
2. identifier must not refer to the same storage area as record-name.
3. the INVALID KEY phrase may not be used with sequentially organised files or RELATIVE files which are accessed sequentially.
4. the INVALID KEY phrase must be specified for all Indexed files and Relative files if access mode is Dynamic or Random.

Function and Effect

The data in record-name, or identifier if specified, is used to replace the data in an existing record on the file associated with record-name. The record replaced depends upon the Organization and Access mode of the file.

a. ORGANIZATION SEQUENTIAL

   The record replaced is the last one read. The last operation upon the file must have been a successful READ.

b. ORGANIZATION INDEXED with ACCESS SEQUENTIAL

   As a. above and the value of the RECORD KEY data item must not have been changed since the READ. The INVALID KEY statement is executed if the RECORD KEY is changed between the READ and the REWRITE.

c. ORGANIZATION INDEXED with ACCESS RANDOM or DYNAMIC

   The record replaced is the one identified by the value of the RECORD KEY data item. The INVALID KEY statement is executed if no record exists with this key value.

d. ORGANIZATION RELATIVE with ACCESS SEQUENTIAL

As a. above.

e. ORGANIZATION RELATIVE with ACCESS RANDOM or DYNAMIC

The record replaced is the one identified by the value of the RELATIVE KEY data item. The INVALID KEY statement is executed if no record exists with a key equal to the value of RELATIVE KEY.

5.31 SEARCH STATEMENT

Format

```
1. SEARCH data-name

        [VARYING { identifier-1   } ]
                 { index-name-1   }

        [AT END imperative-statement-1]

        { WHEN condition { imperative-statement-2 } } ...
        {                { NEXT SENTENCE          } }

2. SEARCH ALL data-name

        [AT END imperative-statement-1]

        WHEN test [AND test] ... { imperative-statement-2 }
                                 { NEXT SENTENCE          }
```

where test is

```
{ identifier-2  { IS EQUAL TO }  { identifier-3          } }
{               { IS =        }  { literal               } }
{                                { arithmetic-expression } }
{ condition-name condition                                 }
```

Note

In the following rules *the table* is used to refer to the table consisting of the occurrences of data-name.

Rules

1. data-name must identify a data item with both OCCURS and INDEXED clauses. For format 2, it must also have the KEY clause. data-name may be qualified.

2. identifier-1 must represent an index data item or a numeric integer data item.
3. condition-name must have only one value.
4. identifier-2 must be referenced by the KEY clause of the table.
5. condition-name must be associated with a data-item which is referenced by the KEY clause of the table.
6. identifier-2 and condition-name must include the first index associated with the table.
7. identifier-3 and identifiers in arithmetic-expression may not be data items referenced by the KEY clause of the table.
8. A data item in the KEY clause of the table may only be referenced by an instance of identifier-2 or condition-name if all the preceding data items in the KEY clause are likewise referenced.

Function and Effect

SEARCH scans the contents of the table for an item which will satisfy one or more specified conditions.

Format 1

This format performs a serial search through the table. This search is under the control of an index-name of the table. If index-name-1 is specified and it is associated with the table then this is the controlling index. In all other cases, the first index-name of the table is the controlling index.

If the value of the controlling index when the search is started is greater than the highest occurrence number valid for the table, the search terminates immediately, and control passes to the next sentence after executing imperative-statement-1 if it is specified. Otherwise the controlling index must have a value which is a valid occurrence number for the table.

Each of the conditions in turn is tested. As soon as one is found to be true, then the corresponding action (imperative-statement-2 or NEXT SENTENCE) is taken. If all the conditions are tested and none found to be true, then:

1. The controlling index is incremented by 1 (equivalent to SET.... UP BY 1).
2. If the VARYING phrase is specified but does not contain the controlling index then identifier-1 or index-name-1 is also incremented:

   If it is a numeric data item – it is incremented by 1.

   If it is an index name – it is incremented to the next occurrence number for its table.

If it is an index data item – it is incremented by the same amount as the controlling index.

3. If the controlling index now has a value which exceeds the highest legal occurrence number for table, the search terminates, imperative-statement-1 is executed (if specified) and control then passes to the next sentence.
4. If the controlling item still identifies an item in the table then processing returns to the testing of the conditions.

Format 2

A non-serial search is made of the whole of table. If no table item can be found to give a true result then imperative-statement-1 is executed (if specified) and control passes to the next sentence. If such an item can be found in the table then the first index name for the table is set to its occurrence number and imperative-statement-2 is executed (if specified) and control passes to the next sentence.

The value of the first index-name for the table, on entry to the statement, is ignored. It will be varied during execution of the statement but will at all times contain a valid occurrence number for table. If the search terminates without having found a suitable table item, then the value of the index name for table is unpredictable.

5.32 SET STATEMENT

Format

1.

```
                                        { identifier-2   }
SET  { identifier-1   ...   }     TO    { index-name-2   }
     { index-name-1   ...   }           { integer-1      }
```

2.

```
SET     index-name-3 ...     { UP BY      }   { identifier-3 }
                             { DOWN BY    }   { integer-2    }
```

Rules

1. identifier-1 and identifier-2 must name either index data items or elementary items described as numeric integers.
2. identifier-3 must be described as a numeric integer.
3. integer-1 must be positive.
4. integer-2 may be positive or negative.

5. In format 1, only the following combinations are valid:

a. an index-name may be set to	index-name index data item integer integer data item
b. an index data item may be set to	index-name index data item
c. an integer data item may be set to	index-name.

Function and Effect

The SET statement is used to place values into index names and data items, to modify index names to refer to different occurrences in a table, and to convert between numeric and index values. The way that values are moved in format 1 is described below.

identifier-1 and index-name-1 are *receiving items*, identifier-2, index-name-2 and integer-1 are *sending items.*

Receiving item	**Sending item**	
index-name	index-name	if for same table, no conversion; if for different table, equivalent occurrence number moved.
index-name	index data item	moved without conversion.
index-name	integer	integer used as occurrence number.
index data item	index data item	no conversion.
index data item	index-name	no conversion.
numeric data item	index-name	index converted to occurrence number.

Format 2 is used to modify the value of an index-name. Both before and after execution of a format 2 SET statement, index-name-2 must contain a valid occurrence number. The occurrence number represented by the index-name is increased or decreased (depending on whether UP or DOWN is specified) by the numeric value specified.

5.33 SORT STATEMENT

Format

```
SORT file-name-1

  { ON { ASCENDING  } KEY data-name... } ...
  {    { DESCENDING }                  }

  { INPUT PROCEDURE IS section-name-1 [ { THRU    } section-name-2 ] }
  {                                   [ { THROUGH }                ] }
  { USING   file-name-2  ...                                         }

  { OUTPUT PROCEDURE IS section-name-3 [ { THRU    }  section-name-4 ] }
  {                                    [ { THROUGH }                 ] }
  { GIVING file-name-3                                                 }
```

Rules

1. file-name-1 must be defined in an SD entry in the Data Division.
2. Each data-name must refer to a data item described within a record associated with file-name-1. It may not have the OCCURS clause nor be subordinate to one. It may not contain an item with the OCCURS clause with the DEPENDING option.
3. If section-name-2 is specified it must come after section-name-1 in the program. Likewise section-name-4 must follow section-name-3.
4. No coding executed from an input or output procedure may be executed from any other part of the program.
5. file-name-2 and file-name-3 must be defined in FD entries in the Data Division.

Function and Effect

The SORT verb takes a set of records, either from specified files or from an input procedure. It then sorts them according to specified criteria and outputs them either to a file or to an output procedure.

Input to the SORT

USING

The file or files specified are read by the SORT and their records are sorted. The files must not be open when the SORT verb is executed. They are opened and closed automatically during the SORT.

INPUT PROCEDURE

The specified procedure is invoked by the SORT statement when it is ready to receive the first input record. When the exit point of the procedure is reached the SORT assumes that there is no further input. While control remains within the INPUT PROCEDURE every record to be included in the SORT must be passed to SORT by execution of a RELEASE statement. This procedure may contain neither SORT nor MERGE statements.

Output from the SORT

GIVING

The SORT statement writes to the specified file the records in the specified sequence. The file is opened and closed automatically by SORT, it must not be open when the SORT verb is executed.

OUTPUT PROCEDURE

The specified procedure is invoked when SORT is ready to produce the sorted output. Each time RETURN is executed a record is passed from the sort to the program. Note that this procedure may contain neither SORT nor MERGE statements. Control returns to the SORT statement after the execution of the last statement in the output procedure.

Specifying the SORT Sequence

The first data-name specified is the most significant key for sorting. Second and subsequent keys are progressively less significant. Comparisons between key values are performed according to normal rules for comparisons. ASCENDING implies lowest key first, DESCENDING the reverse.

Identical Keys

The sequence of output of records with identical key values is unpredictable.

5.34 START STATEMENT – INDEXED FILES

Format

```
START file-name
-----
    [            { EQUAL TO          }              ]
    [            {  -----            }              ]
    [            { =                 }              ]
    [            { GREATER THAN      }              ]
    [ KEY IS     {  -------          }   data-name  ]
    [ ---        { >                 }              ]
    [            { NOT LESS THAN     }              ]
    [            { --- ----          }              ]
    [            { NOT <             }              ]
    [            { ---               }              ]
   INVALID KEY imperative-statement
   -------
```

Rules

1. file-name must be an Indexed file in sequential or dynamic access mode which was opened for INPUT or I–O.
2. data-name may be the RECORD KEY for the file or any alphanumeric data item subordinate to the RECORD KEY starting at its first character position.

Function and Effect

The START statement positions an INDEXED file to a particular record, depending upon the key value specified. If the KEY phrase is not specified, then the RECORD KEY data item is assumed, with a comparison of EQUAL TO. If the KEY phrase is used the specified data item in the disk records is compared with the specified data item in the file section. The file is positioned to the first record whose key satisfies the specified comparison.

If there is no record on file whose key satisfies the comparison then imperative-statement is executed.

5.35 START STATEMENT – RELATIVE FILES

Format

```
START file-name
    [          { EQUAL TO         }            ]
    [          { =                }            ]
    [ KEY IS   { GREATER THAN     }  data-name ]
    [          { >                }            ]
    [          { NOT LESS THAN    }            ]
    [          { NOT <            }            ]
    INVALID KEY imperative-statement
```

Rules

1. file-name must be a Relative file in sequential or dynamic access mode which was opened for INPUT or I–O.
2. If data-name is specified it must be the RELATIVE KEY data item.

Function and Effect

The START statement positions the file to a particular record, depending upon the KEY phrase specified. If no KEY phrase is specified, EQUAL TO is assumed. The file is positioned to the first record whose key satisfies the specified comparison.

If there is no record on the file whose key satisfies the comparison then imperative-statement is executed.

5.36 STOP STATEMENT

Format

STOP RUN

Function and Effect

The STOP statement causes the program to cease execution. Control is normally passed back to the operating system.

5.37 STRING STATEMENT

Format

```
STRING

                                       { identifier-2 }
{ { identifier-1 } ...  DELIMITED BY  { literal-2    }  } ...
  { literal-1    }                     { SIZE         }

   INTO identifier-3 [WITH POINTER identifier-4]

   [ON OVERFLOW imperative-statement]
```

Rules

1. literal-1 and literal-2 may each be a non-numeric literal or a figurative constant (other than ALL).
2. identifier-1, identifier-2 and identifier-3 must reference USAGE DISPLAY data items.
3. identifier-3 must reference an elementary alphanumeric data item without editing symbols or the JUSTIFIED clause.
4. identifier-4 must reference a numeric integer data item which is sufficiently large to contain the length of the data item referenced by identifier-3 plus one. 'P' may not be used in the PICTURE of identifier-4.
5. When identifier-1 or identifier-2 is a numeric data item it must be described as an integer without 'P' in its PICTURE.

Function and Effect

STRING creates a single string in identifier-3 from one or more data items by concatenation.

Each identifier-1 or literal-1 contributes characters to the final result depending on the DELIMITED BY clause following it. If SIZE is specified then all the characters in literal-1 or the data item referenced by identifier-1 are contributed. Otherwise characters are only contributed by literal-1 or identifier-1 up to but excluding the first occurrence of the value specified by identifier-2 or literal-2. If there is no such occurrence then the whole of literal-1 or data item identifier-1 is contributed.

COBOL uses an internal pointer to determine where the destination field (identifier-3) should begin. This value is initialised at 1 unless the WITH POINTER phrase is specified. Identifier-4 will contain the character position in identifier-3 at which the STRING operation begins. When data transfer is complete, COBOL updates the pointer by the number of characters transferred to identifier-3. If the value of identifier-4 is less than 1 or, during execution of the STRING statement, identifier-4 contains a value larger than the size of identifier-3, control is passed to imperative-statement. If the ON OVERFLOW phrase is not specified, control is passed to the next executable statement.

5.38 SUBTRACT STATEMENT

Format

```
1.                 { identifier-1 }
   SUBTRACT        {              } ...   FROM { identifier-2 [ROUNDED] } ...
                   { literal-1    }

       [ON SIZE ERROR imperative-statement]

2.                 { identifier-1 }              { identifier-2 }
   SUBTRACT        {              } ...   FROM   {              }
                   { literal-1    }              { literal-2    }

       GIVING { identifier-3 [ROUNDED] } ...
       [ON SIZE ERROR imperative-statement]
```

For the use of SUBTRACT CORRESPONDING, see CORRESPONDING option – section 6.6.

Rules

1. All literals must be numeric literals.
2. identifier-1 and identifier-2 must be numeric data items.
3. identifier-3 must be a numeric data item or a numeric edited data item.

Function and Effect

The SUBTRACT statement subtracts one or more numeric values from a given numeric value and stores the result in a specified data item or items. The two formats operate differently and so will be considered separately.

In format 1 the values of all identifiers and/or literals between SUBTRACT and FROM are *added* together. The resulting value is then subtracted in turn from each of the identifiers following FROM.

In format 2 the values of all identifiers and/or literals between SUBTRACT and FROM are *added*. The resulting value is then subtracted from the value of the identifier following FROM, and this new result is then moved to each of the identifiers following GIVING (using the normal rules for MOVE).

For the effect of ROUNDED, see section 6.14.

For the effect of ON SIZE ERROR, see section 6.15.

5.39 UNSTRING STATEMENT

Format

```
UNSTRING identifier-1

    [DELIMITED BY [ALL] { identifier-2 } [OR [ALL] { identifier-3 } ]...]
                        { literal-2    }           { literal-3    }

    INTO { identifier-4 [DELIMITER IN identifier-5] [COUNT IN identifier-6] } ...

    [WITH POINTER identifier-7] [TALLYING IN identifier-8]

    [ON OVERFLOW imperative-statement]
```

Rules

1. literal-2 and literal-3 may be non-numeric literals or figurative constants other than ALL. When a figurative constant is specified it stands for a single non-numeric character.
2. identifier-1, identifier-2, identifier-3 and identifier-5 must reference alphanumeric data items.
3. identifier-4 must reference a USAGE DISPLAY data item which is alphabetic (without 'B' in its PICTURE), alphanumeric or numeric (without 'P' in its PICTURE).
4. identifier-6, identifier-7 and identifier-8 must reference numeric integer data items (without 'P' in their PICTUREs).
5. The DELIMITER IN phrase and the COUNT IN phrase may be specified only if the DELIMITED BY phrase is specified.

Function and Effect

UNSTRING takes the contents of a data item (identifier-1) and uses the specified delimiters to divide it into substrings which are then transferred to other data items (identifier-4).

In the description that follows, *delimiter* is used to refer to the contents of identifier-2 or identifier-3, or to literal-2 or literal-3.

The statement executes as follows:

1. If POINTER is not specified, inspection of data item identifier-1 starts with its first character. If POINTER is specified, then inspection starts with the characters whose position is the value of identifier-7. If identifier-7 does not contain a value between 1 and the length of identifier-1 then imperative-statement is executed and no unstringing occurs.

2. Action if DELIMITED is not specified.

   data item identifier-1 is divided into substrings. The first substring starts at the first character to be inspected and is of the same length as the first instance of identifier-4. The second substring starts at the first character following the first substring, and is the same length as the second instance of identifier-4. This continues until the instances of identifier-4 are exhausted or identifier-1 is exhausted.

   If the instances of identifier-4 are exhausted and identifier-1 is not, then:

   a. To each instance of identifier-4 is moved the corresponding substring.

   b. identifier-7, if specified, is incremented by the number of characters examined in identifier-1.

   c. identifier-8, if specified, is incremented by the number of instances of identifier-4.

   d. imperative-statement is executed.

   If identifier-1 is exhausted then:

   a. The appropriate substrings of identifier-1 are moved to the identifier-4 data items. The last identifier-4 to receive a substring may in fact receive a short substring. Standard MOVE rules are followed.

   b. identifier-7, if specified, is incremented by the number of characters transferred from identifier-1.

   c. identifier-8, if specified, is incremented by the number of identifier-4 data-items to which values were moved.

3. Action if DELIMITED is specified.

   As before, identifier-1 is divided into substrings starting from the first character to be inspected. The end of each substring is, however, not fixed by the length of the corresponding identifier-4 but by the occurrence within identifier-1 of one of the delimiters. Each character position in that part of identifier-1 being processed is checked for being the start of a delimiter. The delimiters are taken from left to right. If no delimiter is found to start in that character position then that character is part of a substring. If a delimiter is found to start in that position then the substring comprises all characters from the beginning of the substring up to *but not including* the delimiter. The substring is moved to the appropriate identifier-4 following normal MOVE rules.

If ALL is specified, more than one contiguous occurrence of delimiter is treated as if it were one occurrence.

If DELIMITER is specified for that identifier-4 then the delimiter is moved to identifier-5 unless no delimiter is detected in identifier-1, in which case spaces will be moved to identifier-5.

If COUNT is specified for that identifier-4, then the count of characters inspected, *excluding* the delimiter, is moved into the appropriate identifier-6.

Inspection of identifier-1 restarts, at the first character following the delimiter, to find a substring for the next identifier-4. Note that, as well as having substrings which are longer and shorter than the corresponding identifier-4 data items, it is possible to have a substring of zero length.

This would occur if two adjacent different delimiters were discovered, or if two identical adjacent delimiters were discovered and ALL was not specified. A substring of zero length means that the corresponding identifier-4 will be filled with spaces or zeros (depending on its type), but it will still count as having been assigned a value for purposes of the TALLYING phrase.

5.40 WRITE STATEMENT – INDEXED FILES

Format

```
WRITE record-name [FROM identifier]
        INVALID KEY imperative-statement
```

Rules

1. record-name must be the name of a record associated with an Indexed file which has been opened for OUTPUT or I–O.
2. identifier must not reference the same storage area as record-name.

Function and Effect

This write statement creates a new record on an Indexed file. The key used to identify the record is the content of the data item described in the RECORD KEY clause of SELECT. If FROM is specified a MOVE is performed from identifier to record-name. The data in record-name is then written to the file.

If the file is in sequential access mode and opened for output then the key value should be higher than all keys presently on the file. If this is not so, then imperative-statement is executed. If the file is in random or dynamic access mode, then the key value should not be equal to any key value presently on the file. If it is then imperative-statement is executed.

If an ALTERNATE RECORD KEY without the DUPLICATES phrase is specified and a WRITE would create a record with the same alternate key as some other record then imperative-statement is executed.

5.41 WRITE STATEMENT – PRINTER FILES

Format

```
WRITE record-name [FROM identifier-1]

 [ { BEFORE }            { { identifier-2 }  [ LINE  ] } ]
 [ {        } ADVANCING  { { integer      }  [ LINES ] } ]
 [ { AFTER  }            {                             } ]
 [                       { { mnemonic-name }           } ]
 [                       { { PAGE          }           } ]

 [      { END-OF-PAGE }                        ]
 [  AT  {             }  imperative-statement  ]
 [      { EOP         }                        ]
```

Rules

1. record-name must be the name of a record in a file currently open for OUTPUT or EXTEND.
2. identifier-1 must be the name of a data item (group or elementary) which does not occupy the same area of storage as record-name.
3. identifier-2 must be an elementary integer data item.
4. Neither identifier-2 nor integer may have negative values.
5. mnemonic-name must have been defined in the SPECIAL–NAMES paragraph as referring to some implementor-defined page control feature.

6. mnemonic-name must not be used if the file was defined with the LINAGE clause.
7. The EOP phrase may only be specified if the file was defined with the LINAGE clause.
8. EOP and END–OF–PAGE are synonymous.

Function and Effect

This format of the WRITE statement is used to cause a line to be printed and allow control over the format of the printed page. The basic operation of this WRITE statement is the same as that described for the simple sequential write (section 5.43). The BEFORE, AFTER and AT EOP phrases are extensions concerned with page control.

AFTER ADVANCING Clause

This causes paper movement prior to the transfer of data to form the printed line. If identifier-2 or integer is specified, then the number specified is the number of lines to be moved forward. This movement is relative to the position of the paper prior to the execution of the WRITE. Advancing O lines causes no paper movement. If the ADVANCING phrase is omitted, AFTER ADVANCING 1 is assumed. When mnemonic-name is specified the page advances as specified by the implementor. When PAGE is specified the paper is moved forward so that printing occurs at the top of the next page.

BEFORE ADVANCING Clause

Performs the same function as AFTER (above) but the paper control is performed *after* the printing. This option is rarely used.

Page-end Handling

Action is taken at page end only when the LINAGE clause is specified (see section 4.3) in the File Description entry of the file. The following description is written for the case when AFTER ADVANCING is specified. At the foot of each page one of the following situations will arise:

1. An attempt will be made to write in the footing area using a WRITE statement with the END–OF–PAGE phrase. The line is written and then imperative-statement is executed.
2. An attempt is made to write beyond the current page body. The printer automatically advances to the beginning of the page body of the next page, the line is printed and then imperative-statement is executed if the END–OF–PAGE phrase is specified.

5.42 WRITE STATEMENT – RELATIVE FILES

Format

```
WRITE record-name [FROM identifier]
        INVALID KEY imperative-statement
```

Rules

1. record-name must be the name of a record associated with a Relative file which has been opened for OUTPUT or I–O.
2. identifier must not reference the same storage area as record-name.

Function and Effect

This write statement creates a new record on a Relative file. For sequential access, a new record is written to the file and its relative record number will be placed in the RELATIVE KEY data item (if specified). For random or dynamic access, the record number is given by the value of the RELATIVE KEY data item. If FROM is specified, a MOVE is performed from identifier to record-name. The data in record-name is then written to the file.

If the file is accessed randomly or dynamically then the key value must not be equal to any key value presently on the file. If it is, then imperative-statement is executed.

5.43 WRITE STATEMENT – SEQUENTIAL NON–PRINT FILES

Format

```
WRITE record-name [FROM identifier]
```

Rules

1. record-name must be the name of a record associated with a file currently opened for OUTPUT or EXTEND.
2. identifier must not refer to the same area of storage as record-name.

Function and Effect

The data identified by record-name, or by identifier if it is specified, is used to create a new record on the file identified by record-name.

WRITE A FROM B

is equivalent to

MOVE B TO A

WRITE A.

After execution of a WRITE statement, the data in record-name is no longer available.

6 General

6.1 ARITHMETIC EXPRESSIONS

Format

(operand operator operand [operator operand] ...)

where operator is one of + – * / **

and operand is { numeric-literal | identifier | arithmetic-expression }

Rules

1. identifier must identify a numeric data item.
2. The parentheses may be omitted from the format (but this mav change the meaning of the expression – see parenthesised expressions below).

Function and Effect

An arithmetic expression specifies the operations to be performed, and the data on which they are to be performed, to produce a result. The evaluation of an arithmetic expression proceeds as follows:

1. Expressions without parentheses

   The specified operations are done in the following sequence:

   Exponentiation
   Multiplication and division
   Addition and subtraction

   At each of the three levels of priority, operations are performed from left to right in the expression.

2. Expressions including parentheses

   Conceptually, parenthesised expressions are reduced to non-parenthesised ones by the expedient of evaluating the non-parenthesised sub-expression within the innermost set of parentheses, replacing this set of parentheses and the contained expression by the result of the expression evaluation, and then repeating the procedure until no further parentheses remain.

6.2 CHARACTER SET

The following characters are used for program elements within the COBOL language:

Letters: A B C D ..... Z

Digits: 0 1 2 9

Special Characters

	Space
+	Plus
–	Minus and Hyphen
*	Asterisk
/	Slash
=	Equals Sign
£	Currency Sign
,	Comma
;	Semicolon
.	Full Stop and Decimal Point
"	Quotation marks
(	Left Parenthesis
)	Right Parenthesis
>	Greater Than Sign
<	Less Than Sign

Note

These characters are used in coding a program. The data processed by the program may contain any characters the machine is able to represent.

6.3 COMMENT LINES

Any line containing an asterisk or slash in the indicator area (position 7) is treated as a comment line. Any text in the line will be printed as part of the source listing of the program, but otherwise ignored by the compiler. A comment may continue over several lines, provided that there is an asterisk or slash in each indicator area.

A comment line indicated by an asterisk is printed on the next available line on the printout. One indicated by a slash is printed as the first line on a new page.

6.4 CONDITIONS

Conditions are expressions tested by IF, PERFORM (with UNTIL) and SEARCH statements for "true" or "false" values. They can be considered as simple conditions and combined conditions.

6.4.1 Simple Conditions

These are:

relation conditions

class conditions

sign conditions

condition-name conditions.

6.4.2 Relation Conditions are expressions of the form:

value-1 comparison value-2

where value-1 and value-2 may be identifiers, index-names, literals or arithmetic expressions. Comparison is one of the following:

IS [NOT] GREATER THAN

IS [NOT] LESS THAN

IS [NOT] EQUAL TO

IS [NOT] >

IS [NOT] <

IS [NOT] =

6.4.3 Class Conditions are expressions of the form:

identifier IS [NOT] { NUMERIC | ALPHABETIC }

where identifier must identify a data item with usage DISPLAY.

For a NUMERIC test the data item should have a numeric, numeric edited or alphanumeric picture. A NUMERIC test may be performed on a group item as long as none of the elementary items within it have operational signs. The NUMERIC test checks that the characters within the data item are all digits (0 ... 9) plus a sign in a valid position when the Picture indicates the presence of a sign.

For an ALPHABETIC test the data item referenced must *not* have a numeric picture. The ALPHABETIC test gives a true result if the data item contains only letters (A ... Z) and/or spaces.

6.4.4 Sign Conditions are expressions of the form:

$$\text{arithmetic-expression IS } [\underline{\text{NOT}}] \left\{ \begin{array}{l} \underline{\text{POSITIVE}} \\ \underline{\text{NEGATIVE}} \\ \underline{\text{ZERO}} \end{array} \right\}$$

Representing the arithmetic-expression by A, the sign conditions are equivalent to the following relation conditions:

A POSITIVE $A > 0$

A NEGATIVE $A < 0$

A ZERO $A = 0$

A NOT POSITIVE $A \text{ NOT} > 0$

A NOT NEGATIVE $A \text{ NOT} < 0$

A NOT ZERO $A \text{ NOT} = 0$

6.4.5 Condition-name Conditions are of the form:

$$\text{condition-name} \left[\left\{ \begin{array}{l} \underline{\text{OF}} \\ \underline{\text{IN}} \end{array} \right\} \text{data-name} \right] \ldots \left[\left\{ \begin{array}{l} \underline{\text{OF}} \\ \underline{\text{IN}} \end{array} \right\} \text{file-name} \right]$$
$$[(\text{subscript-1 [subscript-2 [subscript-3])]}$$

condition-name must be defined in a level 88 entry. condition-name is associated with the data item which precedes it and it represents a test or series of tests on this data item. condition-name is true if and only if

1. the data item contains any of the values appearing as literals in the VALUE clause in the condition-name definition

or 2. the data item contains a value between literal-1 and literal-2 for any literal-1 THROUGH literal-2 in the VALUE clause.

Note that the rules for qualification and subscripting are the same as for identifiers.

6.4.6 Combined Conditions

Simple conditions may be combined as follows:

$$\text{simple-condition-1} \left\{ \left\{ \begin{array}{l} \underline{\text{AND}} \\ \underline{\text{OR}} \end{array} \right\} \text{simple-condition-2} \right\} \ldots$$

This combined condition is evaluated by evaluating each AND in turn from left to right and then each OR in turn from left to right. The conditions on either side of each AND are combined to give the value "true" if both conditions are true, and "false" otherwise. The conditions on each side of each OR are combined to give the value "false" if both conditions are false, and "true" otherwise.

Parentheses may be used to override the normal precedence rules (ie ANDs before ORs). When used, the conditions in the innermost parentheses are evaluated first.

A condition of any type may be negated by writing

NOT condition

This is "true" if condition is false and "false" if condition is true. If the negation is to be applied to a combined condition, the combined condition must be placed in parenthesis to indicate the scope of the NOT.

6.5 COPY STATEMENT

Format

```
COPY text-name [ { OF } library-name ]
                 { IN }
    [REPLACING { text-item-1 BY text-item-2 } ...]
```

Rules

1. A COPY statement may occur at any point in a source program except within another COPY statement. It must be preceded by a space and terminated by a period.
2. text-name must be the unique name of a section of source text in a library available to the compiler.
3. If more than one COBOL library is available during compilation, text-name must be qualified by the appropriate library-name.
4. text-item-1 and text-item-2 may each be a single COBOL word, a literal or an identifier or COBOL source text enclosed in double equal signs (eg = = ADD 1 = =). This text must not be null or consist solely of spaces or comment lines.
5. The text retrieved by COPY may not contain any COPY statements.

Function and Effect

The whole of the COBOL source text identified by text-name is incorporated in the program during compilation. This text replaces the COPY statement. If the REPLACING phrase is not specified, the library text is copied into the source program unchanged.

If REPLACING is specified, then the library text is copied with each properly matched text-item-1 replaced by the corresponding text-item-2. text-item-1 matches the library text if the ordered sequence of text words contained in text-item-1 is equal, character for character, to the ordered sequence of library text words. The library text words are examined in turn from left to right and compared against each text-item-1 in turn until a match is found or all comparisons are complete. The library text word, or corresponding replacement, is then copied into the source program and the comparison cycle continues with the next text word.

6.6 CORRESPONDING OPTION

The CORRESPONDING option can be used with three statements: MOVE, ADD and SUBTRACT.

Formats

```
       { CORRESPONDING }
MOVE   {               }   identifier-1 TO identifier-2
       { CORR          }

      { CORRESPONDING }
ADD   {               }   identifier-1 TO identifier-2
      { CORR          }

           { CORRESPONDING }
SUBTRACT   {               }   identifier-1 TO identifier-2
           { CORR          }
```

Rules

1. identifier-1 and identifier-2 must be group items.
2. CORR is an abbreviation for CORRESPONDING.

Function and Effect

The effect of the MOVE CORRESPONDING statement is exactly the same as a sequence of zero or more MOVE statements of the form

```
MOVE item-1 TO item-2
```

for corresponding pairs of item-1 and item-2.

item-1 and item-2 *correspond* with respect to identifier-1 and identifier-2 if all the following conditions hold:

a. item-1 is subordinate to identifier-1.

b. item-2 is subordinate to identifier-2.

c. Neither item-1 nor item-2 are FILLER data items nor level 88 entries.

d. The name of item-1 fully qualified up to but not including identifier-1 is the same as that of item-2 fully qualified up to but not including identifier-2.

e. At least one of item-1 and item-2 is an elementary data item.

The effect of ADD CORRESPONDING (or SUBTRACT CORRESPONDING) is exactly the same as a sequence of zero or more ADD (or SUBTRACT) statements of the form

ADD item-1 TO item-2

(or SUBTRACT item-1 FROM item-2)

for corresponding pairs of item-1 and item-2.

The conditions under which item-1 and item-2 correspond are the same as for MOVE (see above) except that both item-1 and item-2 must be elementary data items. Item-1 and item-2 must both be numeric.

6.7 DEBUGGING LINES

A *debugging line* is a line containing a "D" in the indicator area (column 7).

If the clause WITH DEBUGGING MODE is specified in the Source-Computer paragraph then these lines are compiled normally, as if the "D" was not there, ie the "D" is interpreted as a space.

If the WITH DEBUGGING MODE clause is not specified, then the "D" is interpreted by the compiler as an "*", ie the lines are considered to be comments.

This facility allows statements useful for debugging the program to be left embedded within the source program and then activated/deactivated at compilation time by the simple act of making a small change to the Environment Division. Furthermore if the debugging lines are compiled they can be activated and deactivated at run time.

6.8 IDENTIFIERS

An identifier is a data-name, or a data-name made unique by qualification and/or subscripting.

Format

```
              [ { OF }               ]       [ { OF }            ]
data-name-1   [ {    } data-name-2   ] ...   [ {    }  file-name ]
              [ { IN }               ]       [ { IN }            ]
     [(subscript-1 [subscript-2 [subscript-3] ] )]
```

Rules for Qualification

1. Qualification (that is the OF/IN clause) must be used whenever a data item whose name is not unique is referred to. Sufficient qualification must be used to make the reference unique.
2. data-name-1 and data-name-2 must be subordinate to each data-name-2 that follows them.
3. When file-name is specified data-name-1 must be part of a record definition associated with file-name.
4. One subscript must be used for each OCCURS clause used in the description of the group items containing data-name-1.
5. Each subscript may be one of the following
   - a positive integer
   - the data-name of a numeric data-item which represents an integer
   - an index-name
   - index-name {±} positive-integer
6. index-name must appear in the INDEXED option of an OCCURS clause
7. The value represented by subscript must correspond to an item that exists in the table.

6.9 INDEXED FILES – STATEMENT SUMMARY

ACCESS	OPEN	Permissible statement formats			
SEQUENTIAL	INPUT	READ	[INTO]	AT END	
		START	[KEY]	[INVALID]	
SEQUENTIAL	OUTPUT	WRITE	[FROM]	INVALID	
SEQUENTIAL	I–O	READ	[INTO]	AT END	
		REWRITE	[FROM]	INVALID	
		START	[KEY]	INVALID	
		DELETE			
RANDOM	INPUT	READ	[INTO]	[KEY]	INVALID

RANDOM	OUTPUT	WRITE	[FROM]	INVALID	
RANDOM	I–O	READ	[INTO]	[KEY]	INVALID
		WRITE	[FROM]	INVALID	
		REWRITE	[FROM]	INVALID	
		DELETE	INVALID		
DYNAMIC	INPUT	READ	[INTO]	[KEY]	INVALID
		READ	[NEXT]	[INTO]	AT END
		START	[KEY]	INVALID	
DYNAMIC	OUTPUT	WRITE	[FROM]	INVALID	
DYNAMIC	I–O	READ	[INTO]	[KEY]	INVALID
		READ	[NEXT]	[INTO]	AT END
		WRITE	[FROM]	[INVALID]	
		REWRITE	[FROM]	INVALID	
		START	[KEY]	INVALID	
		DELETE	INVALID		

6.10 LITERALS

A literal is a data item whose value is the same whenever it is referenced. There are three types: numeric literals, non-numeric literals and figurative constants.

Numeric Literals – Rules

These consist of between 1 and 18 digits, optionally with a single decimal point and/or a single sign (+ or –). If a sign is present, it must be the leftmost character in the literal. If no sign is specified, the value is assumed to be positive. If a decimal point is present, it must *not* be the rightmost character. If no decimal point is specified, one is assumed to the right of the rightmost digit.

Non-numeric Literals – Rules

These consist of two quotation marks enclosing between 1 and 120 characters. The characters may be any that the machine can represent except that a quotation mark must be represented by a pair of adjacent quotation marks. (This implies that theoretically one could have 240 characters between the delimiting quotation marks, 120 pairs of quotation marks.)

Figurative Constants

These are standard values referenced through the reserved words below:

ZERO ZEROS ZEROES	A numeric zero or a string of characters zero.
SPACE SPACES	A space character or a string of space characters.
HIGH–VALUE HIGH–VALUES	A string where every character is the highest one in the machine's collating sequence.
LOW–VALUE LOW–VALUES	A string where every character is the lowest one in the machine's collating sequence.
QUOTE QUOTES	A string where every character is the quotation mark ("). Note that QUOTE must *not* be used as the delimiter of a non-numeric literal.
ALL literal	literal should be a normal non-numeric literal (with quotation marks). The figurative constant represents a string of occurrences of literal long enough to fill the context in which the figurative constant is used.

Notes on figurative constants

1. Alternative names, eg QUOTE/QUOTES, mean exactly the same.
2. The length of a figurative constant depends on the context in which it is used. When in an alphanumeric move or compare, it is taken to be the same length as the target or comparand. When used in DISPLAY, STRING or UNSTRING statements, it has a length of 1.
3. ZERO (ZEROS/ZEROES) may be used anywhere that a numeric literal is permitted. Any of the figurative constants (including ZERO) may be used where a non-numeric literal is permitted with the exception of ALL which is not permitted with certain statements as specified in the rules.

6.11 NAMES – CONSTRUCTION RULES

Various names in a COBOL program are created by the programmer. They are

condition-names	mnemonic-names
data-names	paragraph-names
file-names	program-names
implementor-names	record-names
index-names	section-names
library-names	text-names

The following rules govern the construction of these names.

Length

COBOL names must not exceed 30 characters.

Characters

COBOL names may be constructed from letters, digits and hyphens, with the proviso that a hyphen may be neither the first nor the last character. Only paragraph-names and section-names may consist only of digits. Certain names, notably the program-name and the implementor-name in the Select entry, may be further constrained in some implementations.

Uniqueness

All names must either by unique or must be capable of being made unique by qualification.

6.12 PROCEDURE-NAMES

A procedure-name is a section-name, a paragraph-name or a paragraph-name made unique through qualification.

Formats

1. section-name-1

2. paragraph-name [{ <u>OF</u> / <u>IN</u> } section-name-2]

Rules

1. When section-name-2 is specified, paragraph-name must be defined within the section of section-name-2.
2. Qualification (that is the OF/IN clause) must be used whenever a paragraph-name which is not unique is referred to.

6.13 RELATIVE FILES – STATEMENT SUMMARY

ACCESS	OPEN	Permissible statement formats		
SEQUENTIAL	INPUT	READ	[INTO]	AT END
		START	[KEY]	INVALID
SEQUENTIAL	OUTPUT	WRITE	[FROM]	INVALID

SEQUENTIAL	I–O	READ	[INTO]	AT END	
		REWRITE	[FROM]		
		START	[KEY]	INVALID	
		DELETE			
RANDOM	INPUT	READ	[INTO]	INVALID	
RANDOM	OUTPUT	WRITE	[FROM]	INVALID	
RANDOM	I–O	READ	[INTO]	INVALID	
		WRITE	[FROM]	[INVALID]	
		REWRITE	[FROM]	INVALID	
		DELETE	INVALID		
DYNAMIC	INPUT	READ	[INTO]	INVALID	
		READ	[NEXT]	[INTO]	AT END
		START	[KEY]	INVALID	
DYNAMIC	OUTPUT	WRITE	[FROM]	INVALID	
DYNAMIC	I–O	READ	[INTO]	INVALID	
		READ	[NEXT]	[INTO]	AT END
		WRITE	[FROM]	INVALID	
		REWRITE	[FROM]	INVALID	
		START	[KEY]	INVALID	
		DELETE	INVALID		

6.14 ROUNDED OPTION

When a numeric value is assigned to a numeric or numeric edited data item, excess digits on the right are normally truncated, ie lost without trace. Thus a value of 123.45 being assigned to a data item with a picture of 999V9 would give a result of 123.4, and being assigned to a data item with picture 999 would give a result of 123. If the receiving data item is immediately followed by the word ROUNDED then rounding occurs instead of truncation. The effect of rounding is that if the most significant digit being truncated is greater than 4, then the least significant digit remaining is increased by 1.

Note that if ROUNDED and SIZE ERROR are both specified, then rounding is done first.

6.15 SIZE ERROR PHRASE

A size error occurs in an Add, Subtract, Multiply, Divide or Compute statement, when the absolute value of an arithmetic result cannot be moved, correctly aligned, into the appropriate result data item without loss of the most significant digit. It may also occur in a Multiply or Divide statement if an intermediate result exceeds the target size. It will always occur when an attempt is made to divide by zero.

If a size error occurs, the execution of the statement continues with an attempt to assign a value to the next receiving data item, if there is one. All receiving data items to which assignments caused no error receive their correct values. If ON SIZE ERROR was specified, then data items whose assignments caused errors remain unchanged, and the imperative-statement is executed after all assignments have been made. If ON SIZE ERROR was not specified, then the values in these data items are undefined.

Note that if ROUNDED and SIZE ERROR are both specified, then rounding is done first.

7 Reserved Words

The following is the list of reserved words in ANS 74 COBOL:

ACCEPT
ACCESS
ADD
ADVANCING
AFTER
ALL
ALPHABETIC
ALSO
ALTER
ALTERNATE
AND
ARE
AREA
AREAS
ASCENDING
ASSIGN
AT
AUTHOR

BEFORE
BLANK
BLOCK
BOTTOM
BY

CALL
CANCEL
CD
CF
CH
CHARACTER
CHARACTERS
CLOCK–UNITS
CLOSE
COBOL
CODE
CODE–SET
COLLATING
COLUMN
COMMA
COMMUNICATION
COMP
COMPUTATIONAL
COMPUTE
CONFIGURATION
CONTAINS
CONTROL
CONTROLS
COPY
CORR
CORRESPONDING
COUNT
CURRENCY

DATA
DATE
DATE–COMPILED
DATE–WRITTEN
DAY
DE
DEBUG–CONTENTS
DEBUG–ITEM
DEBUG–LINE
DEBUG–NAME
DEBUG–SUB–1
DEBUG–SUB–2
DEBUG–SUB–3
DEBUGGING
DECIMAL–POINT
DECLARATIVES
DELETE
DELIMITED
DELIMITER
DEPENDING
DESCENDING
DESTINATION
DETAIL
DISABLE
DISPLAY
DIVIDE
DIVISION
DOWN
DUPLICATES
DYNAMIC

EGI
ELSE
EMI
ENABLE
END

END-OF-PAGE
ENTER
ENVIRONMENT
EOP
EQUAL
ERROR
ESI
EVERY
EXCEPTION
EXIT
EXTEND

FD
FILE
FILE-CONTROL
FILLER
FINAL
FIRST
FOOTING
FOR
FROM

GENERATE
GIVING
GO
GREATER
GROUP

HEADING
HIGH-VALUE
HIGH-VALUES

I-O
I-O-CONTROL
IDENTIFICATION
IF
IN
INDEX
INDEXED
INDICATE
INITIAL
INITIATE
INPUT
INPUT-OUTPUT
INSPECT
INSTALLATION
INTO
INVALID
IS

JUST
JUSTIFIED

KEY

LABEL
LAST
LEADING
LEFT
LENGTH
LESS
LIMIT
LIMITS
LINAGE
LINAGE-COUNTER
LINE
LINE-COUNTER
LINES
LINKAGE
LOCK
LOW-VALUE
LOW-VALUES

MEMORY
MERGE
MESSAGE
MODE
MODULES
MOVE
MULTIPLE
MULTIPLY

NATIVE
NEGATIVE
NEXT
NO
NOT
NUMBER
NUMERIC

OBJECT-COMPUTER
OCCURS
OF
OFF
OMITTED
ON
OPEN
OPTIONAL
OR
ORGANIZATION
OUTPUT
OVERFLOW

PAGE
PAGE-COUNTER
PERFORM
PF
PH
PIC
PICTURE
PLUS
POINTER
POSITION
POSITIVE
PRINTING
PROCEDURE
PROCEDURES
PROCEED
PROGRAM
PROGRAM-ID

QUEUE
QUOTE
QUOTES

RANDOM
RD
READ
RECEIVE

RECORD
RECORDS
REDEFINES
REEL
REFERENCES
RELATIVE
RELEASE
REMAINDER
REMOVAL
RENAMES
REPLACING
REPORT
REPORTING
REPORTS
RERUN
RESERVE
RESET
RETURN
REVERSED
REWIND
REWRITE
RF
RH
RIGHT
ROUNDED
RUN

SAME
SD
SEARCH
SECTION
SECURITY
SEGMENT
SEGMENT-LIMIT
SELECT
SEND
SENTENCE
SEPARATE
SEQUENCE
SEQUENTIAL
SET
SIGN
SIZE
SORT
SORT-MERGE
SOURCE
SOURCE-COMPUTER
SPACE
SPACES
SPECIAL-NAMES
STANDARD
STANDARD-1
START
STATUS
STOP
STRING
SUB-QUEUE-1
SUB-QUEUE-2
SUB-QUEUE-3
SUBTRACT
SUM
SUPPRESS
SYMBOLIC
SYNC
SYNCHRONIZED

TABLE
TALLYING
TAPE
TERMINAL
TERMINATE
TEXT
THAN
THROUGH
THRU
TIME
TIMES
TO
TOP
TRAILING
TYPE

UNIT
UNSTRING
UNTIL
UP
UPON
USAGE
USE
USING

VALUE
VALUES
VARYING

WHEN
WITH
WORDS
WORKING-STORAGE
WRITE

ZERO
ZEROES
ZEROS

*
-
/
**
>
<
=

Index

For the convenience of the reader, a combined index for this book and its companion volume – *COBOL Programming* – is provided. The reader is reminded that the entries for *COBOL Programming* are of a conceptual and introductory nature, whilst those for the *Reference Summary* provide more complete and factual information on the individual features of COBOL.